SO, YOU WANT TO BE A PILOT, EH?

So, You Want to be a Pilot, Eh?

A Guidebook for Canadian Pilot Training

James Ball, B.A., CPL

Part of the Writing on Stone
Canadian Career Series

Writing On Stone Press
PO Box 259, Raymond, AB T0K 2S0
(403) 752-4800
www.writingonstone.ca

Published by:
Writing on Stone Press Inc.
P.O. Box 259
Raymond, Alberta, Canada T0K 2S0
(403) 752-4800
Fax: (403) 752-4815
Email: info@writingonstone.ca
Web: http://www.writingonstone.ca

ISBN 0-9781309-1-X

Edited by KJ Turner and Julianne Geiger

LIBRARY AND ARCHIVES CANADA
CATALOGUING IN PUBLICATION

Ball, James, 1979-
So, You Want to be a Pilot, Eh? : A Guidebook for Canadian
Pilot Training / James Ball. —1st ed.

(Writing on Stone Canadian Career Series)
ISBN 978-0-9781309-1-6

1. **Airplanes--Piloting--Vocational guidance--Canada. 2. Flight**
training--Canada. I. Title. II. Series.

TL561.B34 2007   629.132'520971   C2007-905040-9

To all my friends and family that have supported me on this journey, and to the ex-K9 folks still 'Living The Dream.'

TABLE OF CONTENTS

FOREWORD

L IKE many of you, my aviation career began at the end of a runway watching planes land and take off. Many aspiring pilots fall in love with the dream of flying. Deciding to start a career based on a dream can sound romantic however as attractive as the dream may seem it requires sober thought considering all the facts.

Deciding to fly as a recreation can be one of life's most fulfilling aspects. Deciding to fly as a career is an important life decision, which should be made after studying a book such as this and considering all the facts and issues. While I urge you not to make this decision based on a dream, if you do choose to fly never lose the passion for flying that ignited the dream.

Too many pilots who have a number of years experience admit too late that they made a mistake because they fell in love with the concept of being an airline captain and didn't understand what they were getting into. As a career, piloting can be the best job in the world for some while it can represent frustration for others.

In addition to reading this book, talk to as many career professionals as you can and then, and only then, decide for yourself if this is your chosen vocation. Get used to the idea you may not end up in the exact job you aspired to. Your schedule and lifestyle may not exactly resemble the stories of fifteen days off a month and the high salaries of a decade ago that have been adjusted downward. If you find that you love flying and have eyes open wide, and can accept the compromises of the lifestyle for yourself and your family, then a piloting career may very well be just right for you.

As I look back on my career I know I picked the right job because I still love to fly and I love my job. I am living the dream! I can assure you that if you do your homework well and decide to become a career pilot for the right reasons, then you will succeed beyond your dreams and you will love what you are doing. Perhaps looking back you will decide that you never really worked at all!

Russ Payson
Chairman and CEO
Skyservice

A Boeing 767 on Final Approach
Photo by Adam Van Dusen

CHAPTER ONE: OPENING THOUGHTS

In a world full of people, only some want to fly.
Isn't that crazy?

—Seal, 'Crazy'

So, You Want to be a Pilot

S O you think you might want to be a pilot, eh? Perhaps you want to be an airline pilot and the thought of traveling the world and handling a big jet sounds like an exciting future. Or maybe you'd like to fly water bombers in remote areas of Canada. Maybe you'd like to fly the rich and famous around the world in a private business jet. Being a pilot can be a diverse, challenging, and rewarding career. However, becoming one is not an easy task. There are many different routes one can take to become a pilot. In fact, if you ask several pilots, you will likely find that each of them followed a unique path to get to where they are now.

When I first started out in the aviation industry, I had no idea what to expect. Although there are a number of books to help one obtain their pilot licence in Canada, they do not fully address the complexities of how to succeed in such a stringent industry. I have known people who had dreamed of becoming a pilot and yet quit somewhere along the way. It is my hope that this book will help you decide if a career as a pilot is right for you, and if so, that it will aid you in your journey down that path.

This book will initially look at the basics of obtaining your licences. Later sections will offer information on finding that ever-elusive first job. Even if you're already on the road to becoming a pilot, much of the information in this book will still be of great value to you. One of the key aspects to becoming a pilot is making the best decisions based on the information available. And that's what this book is all about—providing information so that you can make informed decisions.

Purpose

The purpose of this book is to acquaint you with the various paths that you can take in order to become a pilot, and the various required steps in each. This book *is not* intended to sell the idea of becoming a pilot, nor is it intended to scare you away. I've spoken with many pilots during my aviation career and while writing this book, and opinions have varied. Some I've spoken with love every second of their job and cannot fathom the idea of doing anything else. Some enjoy their work the majority of the time but confess to having days where they wish they were doing something else, and others truly dislike what they're doing and continue to work a job they dislike due to financial commitments or other life factors. It's my hope that this book will influence those people interested in a career in aviation to investigate further. At the same time, I also hope to highlight the various difficulties and challenges one might face on the road to becoming a pilot.

Much of this book is opinion. Although you're required to obtain specific licences and ratings to become a pilot, there are numerous routes that can be taken to obtain them. Some routes are better than others in achieving that goal. Similarly, there is no one way to get a job. Although the options are many, by talking to different pilots who have landed jobs (no pun intended) as well as Chief Pilots who have been responsible for hiring, I have attempted to show what works and what does not work. Other pilots may have different opinions about numerous topics in this book, and there's nothing wrong with that; I encourage you to find out as much information as possible from as many sources as possible. Digest the information contained in this book and then form your own opinions.

Why I Wrote This Book

Throughout my career, both in and out of aviation, I have heard so many varying opinions and thoughts about what it must be like to be a pilot. I've heard non-pilots express the wish that they had simply given in to their dreams and pursued flight training. I've heard pilots express the wish that they'd done something else with their lives or taken a different path to get to where they are today. One of the biggest motivations for writing this book was the high number of people who start their flight training only to fall short of completion. Flight training is challenging and expensive, and finding a first flying job can be an even tougher challenge. It's valuable to know what you're getting yourself into.

When I was considering a pilot career, I asked a few people the question, "How does someone become a pilot in Canada?" It turns out the answers were far more complex than I expected. There are books out there that cover the basics: get a licence and get a job. But even those two tasks can prove to be complex. For example, you may ask, "What's the best way to get your licences?" or "How does one find that first job?" Too often, I've heard pilots lament that if they had only known X or Y they would have done things differently.

Some portions of this book may seem slightly pessimistic at first. The cautionary tone is derived from feedback passed down to me from current pilots who think, "I wish I'd known that before I'd started." However, I want to stress that being a pilot IS a really cool job! Airline pilots are in control of a multi-million dollar, state-of-the-art piece of technology that's flying hundreds of people 800 km/h, ten kilometres above the earth's surface! They get to visit places that most people only dream of seeing, meet incredible and interesting people and, best of all, experience the thrill of flight. They get to experience all this while enjoying the best office view in the world (except for maybe an Astronaut—but most Astronauts started as pilots anyway, and technically, their office is out of this world).

The Canadian Aviation Industry

For most Canadians, their idea of the Canadian aviation industry involves only the larger scheduled airlines such as Air Canada and WestJet. Some may also be aware of charter airlines such as Skyservice and Air Transat, who focus mostly on vacation flights to Caribbean and European destinations. The rest of the industry is usually labelled generally as "small planes." However, these small planes have functions that are as diverse as the pilots who fly them. In Canada, there are a number of categories of aviation businesses, and if you're thinking about becoming a pilot, a basic understanding of each of the different categories will prove helpful.

The first thing that needs mentioning is a pet peeve of almost all pilots: The use of the term "commercial pilot" when referring exclusively to airline pilots. This term actually includes a much wider group of pilots, including any pilot flying planes for a living. It doesn't matter if you're flying a Boeing 767, or a small single engine Cessna—if you're getting paid to do it, you're a commercial pilot. A question common to the ears of any pilot flying non-airline planes, usually asked by a well-meaning but misinformed passenger, is, "So, do you want to be a commercial pilot someday?" Although this question never really bothered me, it is worth remembering that some pilots might be offended by the misuse of this job title.

As discussed earlier, the most widely known category of aviation in Canada is the scheduled and charter airlines. These airlines carry the bulk of passengers to and from the larger cities in Canada, and international destinations around the world. These carriers, often referred to as "mainline carriers," operate a range of larger airliners, from the fifty-seat Bombardier Regional Jet to the 270-seat Airbus A340. While WestJet exclusively uses the Boeing 737, other airlines use varying types of aircraft in their fleet. For example, Air Canada's mainline fleet of 200 aircraft currently consists of eleven different types (although some are merely different versions or stretched models of the same plane), and Skyservice operates four types of aircraft.

For city pairs where the passenger load does not require planes of that size, regional airlines utilize smaller jets and turboprops to provide air service. The largest regional airline in Canada is Air

Canada's regional subsidiary Jazz, which has a fleet of 135 aircraft. This fleet includes a fifty to seventy-five-seat Bombardier Regional Jet and the thirty-seven to fifty-seat Dash-8 turboprop. There are a few regional airlines that are not owned by mainline carriers, such as Calm Air and Pacific Coastal. However, even these stand-alone regional airlines oftentimes have code-share agreements with the larger airlines, which allow flights to be booked through Air Canada for travel on the regional carrier. Smaller regional carriers—such as Central Mountain Air, Bearskin Airlines, and Air Labrador—operate between even smaller cities with smaller planes, such as the nineteen-seat Beech 1900D or the Fairchild Metro.

Canada has an active air cargo industry in which packages and parcels are delivered quickly across the country and around the world. The corporate structure of the air cargo industry is very intricate. Most parcels are shipped using one of the larger courier companies such as FedEx, UPS, or Purolator. In the US, these courier companies actually operate their own aircraft flying between US cities. Between Canadian cities, however, the courier companies will contract a cargo airline to fly their parcels for them. These airlines—such as CargoJet, MorningStar, and the cargo division of Kelowna Flightcraft—use older airliners (usually Boeing 727s) to fly overnight cargo between the larger cities in Canada. They will also make connections at various airports for cargo to be transferred to other planes for delivery into the US. For delivery between smaller cities, (Hamilton, Ottawa, and Kingston, for example) courier companies look to even smaller cargo operators such as SkyLink Express and Georgian Express to fly these routes using Beech 1900, Cessna Caravan, and other similar planes.

A Kelowna Flightcraft Boeing 727
Photo by Adam Van Dusen

All other aircraft uses are usually grouped under the broad heading "General Aviation" and include business aviation, charter and smaller scheduled service, ad hoc cargo service, air ambulance service, and aerial services such as sight seeing, crop dusting, and flight training. The business aviation sector in Canada is much smaller than that in the US—however, some of the larger companies in Canada will operate a corporate flight department so upper management can travel efficiently to remote destinations at odd hours. Business aircraft range from smaller turboprops such as the Beechcraft King Air or Pilatus PC-12, to the larger business jets, such as the Falcon 900 or Gulfstream 450. Some companies will operate their flight department "in-house," which means that they are personally responsible for all management responsibilities. Others will contract out that service to an aircraft management company. In the latter case, the corporation will pay for the plane while the management company looks after all the details of managing the aircraft, such as staffing and maintenance.

You will likely start your first flying job in one of the other sections of general aviation in Canada. Flight training schools will usually have a fleet comprised of single-engine aircraft such as a Cessna 150 or 172, and one or two small multi-engine planes such as a Piper Seminole. These planes are used for both flight training, rentals, and small charter or sightseeing flights.

Another potential first job may be with a small charter airline. These companies typically offer a range of aviation services such as charters, cargo flights, scheduled flights, and medevacs. The number of services offered by these companies varies widely. Some have only one or two special-use planes, and others have a variety of planes offering many different services. Charter flights, in this sense, differ slightly from the larger charter airlines. Charter flights serve customers who require the use of an aircraft (usually a smaller one), when buying a ticket for an airline will not suffice. This type of charter operation, called Air Taxi, is essentially the equivalent of the customer using the aircraft as their own personal taxicab. Some trips may be simple flights from point A to point B, while others are often multi-destination trips, the purpose of which can vary dramatically.

Medevac, or air ambulance operations, are an important aviation service. There are different types of air ambulance operations, each with different purposes. International air ambulance companies are involved in the transfer of patients between different countries, most often for insurance companies. A typical use of an international medevac would be for an injured tourist who needs to be transferred back to their home country. On a local scale, air ambulance flights (airplane) are often used when a patient in a smaller community requires healthcare services that are only available in larger cities. An air ambulance offers a quick and convenient way to transfer the patient. Helicopter air ambulances are often used in a similar capacity, but can also be used for emergency transfers of critical patients, such as patients who have been badly injured in a car accident.

There are still many other types of aviation services. Some companies, specifically those near tourist destinations (Niagara Falls, for example), offer sightseeing tours over the local area. And in rural areas, a very popular and efficient way to distribute pesticides over a large area of land is with the use of crop-spraying planes. Across

Canada and around the world, aerial photography and geo-surveying companies offer unique ways to view the earth. Water bombing and aerial firefighting operations are key defensive strategies in combating forest fires. These services and others are made possible by the aviation industry.

Military Aviation is a truly unique venture. An entire book could be written about the different operations and the various aircraft the military employs. The Canadian military operates a broad range of helicopters and aircraft. The new Cormorant Helicopter acts as a nautical search-and-rescue aircraft, whereas the Gryphon Helicopter is typically used to assist ground-combat operations. The Air Force also operates a wide variety of fixed-wing (airplanes) aircraft. The largest are a fleet of Airbus A310s, which operate as crew transport. Other planes include the Bombardier Challengers (one of which operates as the Prime Minister's personal plane), the C-130 Hercules that is used in numerous roles such as search-and-rescue and transport, and the CF-18 Hornet fighter jet. For more information about the Canadian Air Force, check out http://www.airforce. forces.gc.ca/.

Career Paths

The road to becoming a pilot is a long one, and can take many different paths. It would be nearly impossible for someone to accomplish every job on the following list. There are different options for gaining experience in the aviation industry. The following list is an example of some options grouped together. Even within the groups, it is *not* imperative that you hit each individual step. This list provides a general idea of some of the steps involved in obtaining your licences and working for an airline or corporate flight department.

Intro Flight
Training with an instructor
Solo
Private Licence
Night rating
Commercial Licence

Instructor's rating
Class IV instructor
Class III instructor
Class II instructor
Class I instructor

Float rating
Working the dock
Flying single-engine float planes
Flying multi-engine float planes

Multi-IFR rating
Working the ramp
First officer on a multi-engine plane
Captain on a single-engine plane
Captain on a small multi-engine plane

Regional Airline
First officer with a regional airline
Captain with a regional airline

Corporate Flight Department
First Officer on a corporate jet
Captain on a corporate jet

Major Airline
First Officer with a major airline
Captain with a major airline

Types of Certifications

One doesn't simply complete their flight training and become a 747 Captain. There are a flurry of licences, ratings, and permits that one must combine with experience and seniority to become an airline Captain or senior pilot. In fact, it's difficult to keep track of all the different licences and ratings that are available to pilots. It can be even more difficult to pay for them all.

When you begin training, you must first obtain a student pilot permit, which allows you to legally fly solo during daylight hours within Canada. To obtain this permit, a number of requirements must be met. You must (a) be over fourteen years of age; (b) pass a short, written test, known as "PSTAR"; (c) have and present a valid form of I.D. such as a passport, or a birth certificate; and (d) secure the appropriate medical certification (see next chapter).

While most students choose to obtain a private pilot licence, there is another option available with fewer prerequisites, and therefore is quicker and less expensive to obtain. A Recreational Pilot Permit, or "The Rec," allows you to fly within Canada during daylight hours carrying one passenger. This is not considered a full licence and *is not recognized internationally*. You must be over sixteen to receive this type of permit. Individual flight schools will impose weather restrictions and other conditions on pilots who hold this permit.. But despite the limitations, The Rec is a quicker and less expensive option for those satisfied with short, recreational flights, such as taking a friend flying near your local airport. On a side note, it's also a great way to impress a date. I know a few pilots who, after taking a potential girlfriend or boyfriend flying for their first date, ended up marrying them! (Don't get into aviation for this reason alone, though.)

Unlike a pilot *permit*, a pilot *licence* is recognized internationally, and various ratings can be added to a licence, resulting in less restriction with each addition. The entry-level licence is the private pilot licence, which allows a pilot to fly by themselves and with passengers, but not for hire. The basic private licence is for flying single-engine, non-high performance land airplanes. This licence is most useful for those who have no intention of working as a pilot, but wish to fly friends around in a self-owned or rented plane, perhaps from a flying club. This licence is also the usual stepping-stone for those desiring a commercial licence. To obtain a private licence, you must be over seventeen, have at least a Class 3 medical certificate, and pass a written exam and a flight test. Since this licence has international recognition, it allows you to fly not only in Canada, but also across the border into the US. If you do this, be sure you have the proper documentation and are familiar with the process of flying across the border. You don't want to show up in a small plane, unannounced, without the proper documents. Although you cannot fly for hire or reward with a private licence, there are still ways to gain flight hours with a private licence. The easiest way is to take friends up on sightseeing flights, or perhaps take advantage of the opportunities in the non-profit sector—giving rides to air cadets, or towing planes for gliding clubs, for example.

The next licence after a private licence is a commercial pilot licence. To gain a commercial licence you must have, at a minimum, 200 hours of flight time. You must be over the age of eighteen, and pass a written exam and a flight test. If you wish to work as a pilot and receive payment for flying, the commercial licence is the minimum requirement—and building hours is a lot easier when someone is paying you to do it.

You can add various ratings to both a commercial licence and a private licence in order to become eligible to fly other types of planes in a variety of conditions. These include a float rating, a multi-engine rating, an instrument rating, an instructor's rating, and for those with only a private licence, a night rating. There's also the option of the rare "VFR over the top" rating, which allows non-instrument-rated pilots to fly without reference to the ground, "over the top" of clouds.

It's not necessary to obtain every rating. Depending on your flying preference, it may only be necessary to obtain a few ratings. For example, if you want to be a bush pilot flying float planes, then it's obviously necessary to get a float rating. If, on the other hand, you never want to be an instructor, it wouldn't make much sense to obtain an instructor's rating. I will go into more detail about the pros and cons of different routes in Chapter 6.

The Airline Transport Pilot Licence (ATPL) is the highest class of licence that a pilot can achieve. The ATPL allows a pilot to fly as a Captain on larger aircraft that have a maximum take-off weight of over 12,500 lbs. This generally includes all planes that have more than fifteen to nineteen seats. It takes many years of flying to become eligible for an APTL (co-pilot flights can only count towards half of this requirement). Other experience-related requirements are also necessary, each with a specified number of hours. These include cross-country hours, night hours, and time as pilot-in-command (acting as captain) as well as successfully completing two written tests.

What Pilots Do

The role of a pilot can seem straightforward—they are the person who flies the plane. Nevertheless, a pilot's duties are much more complicated than sitting up front and making the plane go. There are a number of responsibilities and duties that pilots have before the flight, during the flight, after the flight, and between flights.

Flying involves detailed and disciplined preparation. Unlike driving a car (just hop in, start it, and go!), each flight requires extensive pre-flight planning and preparation. Although different pilot jobs have varying levels of responsibility regarding pre-flight planning and preparation, it is ultimately the Captain's duty to ensure that the planning is satisfactory. Flight planning is an important responsibility for a pilot. Before a flight leaves, usually long before the passengers have arrived, the pilot (or dispatcher in larger airlines) will have (1) checked the weather en-route and at the destination, (2) picked the route that they are going to take, (3) calculated the quantity and weight of the fuel required, (4) calculated a weight and balance for the passengers and cargo, (5) completed a pre-flight inspection of the aircraft, (6) talked to the maintenance engineers about the aircraft regarding anything that has recently been fixed, and (7) discussed pertinent issues with other employees of the airline.

Before take-off, airline pilots will complete numerous pre-flight preparations. This preparation includes entering the flight plan into the Flight Management System (FMS), copying and reading back their Air Traffic Control clearance to make ATC aware of the plans, briefing passengers and crew, and staying in touch with their company dispatch. Different levels of aviation will have different pre-flight checks. For example, most of the smaller charter planes do not have an FMS, and therefore the pilot has the added responsibility of keeping track of the plane's route and location. The routes of these smaller planes are, however, usually less complex and significantly shorter than the routes of the larger airliners.

The Flight Deck of a Pilatus PC-12
Photo by Adam Van Dusen

In flight, the pilots (specifically the Captain) are responsible for the safety of the aircraft and its passengers. This involves not only diligently following all standard operating procedures, but also successfully dealing with any emergencies or abnormalities during the flight. Normal in-flight procedures are much more complicated than simply "kicking the tires & lighting the fires!" It seems that there is a checklist for everything. Checklists must be followed before you start, before you taxi, before you take off, before you level off, before you begin your descent, before you land, after you land, and during shut down of the aircraft. The rigorous process of adhering to checklists can seem somewhat strange to non-pilots. In the smaller planes that I flew, passengers were able to see what I was doing. When they noticed me referencing a checklist, some of them have asked me if I actually knew how to fly. And if I do know how to fly, then why did I need to follow instructions!? The truth is, checklists are completely normal and are a vital part of everyday flying. Checklists are useful tools that ensure every task is completed. They also improve communication between crewmembers. In flight, it's also important to be "ahead of the airplane." Whether or not the plane is on autopilot, pilots have much to anticipate: what heading they'll be flying on; what air traffic control radio frequency they may need to change; what altitude they must reach; the different instrument approaches they'll need to fly. Unlike a car, if you miss your turn, you can't back up and make a U-turn in the sky.

Before, during, and after a flight, a pilot must be a problem-solver. In both normal operations and emergency conditions, the pilot is responsible for finding the best solution to various difficulties encountered en-route. Flying is a complex endeavour. You not only have to fly the aircraft safely, but you also have to do so while taking into consideration the needs of your passengers, the needs of your company, air traffic control instructions, and the weather. Numerous abnormal situations will inevitably arise in the course of the job. It is the pilot's job to resolve all issues that may prevent your passengers from arriving at their destination safely and on time. Sometimes that requires thinking "outside the box."

After landing, the pilots must ensure the plane is in fit condition to make its next flight. If maintenance issues were encountered during the flight, pilots must inform both the aircraft maintenance engineers on the ground and the company dispatch. It is also helpful if they can anticipate potential problems that may affect the next flight and bring it to the attention of the airline. While pilots are not expected to have all the answers, they are expected to be team players and assist in problem solving.

Even when not flying, pilots need to be preparing themselves for their next flight. Pilots have to pay attention to how much sleep they have had and when they last consumed alcohol. They also have to constantly review emergency procedures and keep up with the latest training methods, which change frequently. They must also meet the requirements in check rides, which they will undergo from time to time to ensure their skill level has not dropped.

There is an excellent book entitled: "From the Flight Deck: Plane Talk and Sky Science" by Doug Morris that gives a great explanation of the different aspects of an airline flight while answering questions that many passengers likely have had while flying. Doug Morris is an airline pilot and certified meteorologist who writes a monthly column in Air Canada's in-flight magazine and in this book, he explains everything from a brief introduction to the physics of flight, to how aircraft work, to how pilots spend their time during layovers. It's worth the read to gain a good understanding of some of the basics of airline flying.

My Story

To begin, I think it would be a good idea to give my experience in aviation. I'm sure many pilots have such stories, but each is unique. I highly recommend asking pilots you come in contact with why they decided to become a pilot. It often results in an interesting story, and can give you an idea of what to expect. This should be easy—pilots love to talk about flying!

When I was young, my Dad would take me to the airport to watch the planes land. And I always enjoyed going on plane rides for vacation. But it never really occurred to me that I could become a pilot. I guess I assumed that you had to join the military, or be a float pilot in the bush for half your life first. During my last year of high school, I still didn't know what I wanted to do with my life. I later decided to study business, and I applied to a handful of universities. After taking OAC (grade 13 in Ontario) Economics for a few months, my excitement for business disappeared! My aunt, who was an Air Canada flight attendant, had recently married an Air Canada pilot. At a family gathering, I asked him how someone becomes a pilot. He told me about various college aviation programs that specialize in flight training in Canada, and suggested that I come along on a flight with him and sit up in the flight deck of the Airbus A320 that he was flying at the time.

A few weeks later, I sat in the jump seat as we flew from Toronto to Newark, NJ. We stayed at the World Trade Center Marriott hotel and spent the day sightseeing in Manhattan. We flew back to Toronto the next day, and I was hooked! I applied to Seneca College in Toronto for their Aviation & Flight Technology Program, and discovered that I needed to pick up grade 12 physics. After completing this course in night school, I was accepted to Seneca. At the time (it has since changed), Seneca's program included a year of "pre-aviation," which included two semesters of straight academic work and absolutely no flight training. They let 154 people into the first year program, but only the top thirty-seven continued to the second year to begin flight training. I worked hard and thankfully made the cut. Flight training was great! It was exciting, challenging, and nerve-wracking—all at the same time.

In the summer of 2001, after three years at Seneca, I graduated with my Commercial Pilot Licence and Multi-Engine IFR rating. Now I needed to find a job.

Although the events of 9/11 had not yet transpired, the aviation industry had already started to slow down. Operators hiring new, low-time pilots were scarce. After some thought, I decided to take a road-trip and hand out résumés to various air operators in more remote parts of the country. I didn't get a job at the time, but I decided to take my friend's advice and move to Thompson, MB, in hopes of getting a job with an airline that was based there and that hired low-time pilots. Moving was a big culture shock. I had lived in Toronto my entire life, and now I was in a small, isolated town in Northern Manitoba, where it seemed that everybody knew everybody.

In Thompson, I got a job working at a grocery store. This was *not* my ideal job after just graduating from college. However, it provided enough money for food, so I took it. After working at the grocery store for three months, I was offered a job as a ramp attendant (a.k.a. rampie or ramp rat) at the airline. I spent fifteen months working on the ground; loading bags, setting up seats, cleaning, and trying to make a good impression. It was hard work. Even harder when you consider that winters in Thompson are really cold. There were mornings where I went to work outside and it was -42° C! The good thing about working on the ramp was that I was working with other potential pilots who were in the same position as me. Although the work was hard, we all tried to have fun and to remember why we were there.

The hard work paid off. My first flying position was as a First Officer on a Cessna Conquest II, flying Medevacs (Air Ambulance flights) to the various reserves in Northern Manitoba and some of the communities in the Keewatin District of Nunavut, on the west coast of Hudson Bay. Medevacs were extremely interesting. Each flight was different, and most of the time you had no idea where and when you would be flying until half an hour before each flight. The Conquest was a great first plane to fly, and each of the different

Captains I flew with had different things to teach me. I learned a lot about flying, and a lot about myself.

Cessna C441 Conquest II
photo by James Ball

My next position was as a Captain on a Cessna 206 & 207, flying charters and cargo flights in Northern Manitoba. Unlike the Conquest, which flew at high speeds and high altitudes, the single-engine Cessnas were "low and slow." The flights I flew were into some of the same reserves I had flown into before, but also included flights into remote hunting and fishing lodges. Some of the runways were in very poor condition, and there were often rocks or trees very close to the edge. This was very different from some of the large international airports in big cities such as Toronto or Calgary. Flying around Northern Manitoba by myself presented many challenges, including loading heavy cargo on and off the plane—often alone. This cargo would include everything from pop and chips, to oil drums and dead bodies!

For a number of reasons that will be discussed in the *backup plan* section in the next chapter, I decided to return to school to obtain a degree. Two months after I left my airline, they went out of business, reinforcing my belief that it is a good idea to have a backup plan. I obtained my bachelor degree and am now attending law school. Since returning to school, I continue to work part-time in the aviation industry.

Outline

I've attempted to outline this book by following the basic steps you are likely to encounter on the road to becoming a pilot. It's my hope that this book will serve as an overview of what's required to become a pilot, and will give you information that will help make the journey easier. If you already have your private licence, you may ignore the section that explains the flight test for a private pilot licence. However, there are general tips in each section that can be applied to other levels of your flight training or flying career. I would recommend that you at least skim through each chapter, even if you think you have already passed that point in your flying career. You may stumble on a good tip that you can apply later, or at least pass on to someone else who is on the road to becoming a pilot.

Throughout this book, I've included a number of *Hangar Talk* sections, where you'll find various comments, thoughts, and words of advice from other pilots in the industry. The first one includes thoughts on the various reasons for becoming a pilot.

Hangar Talk – Why Did You Become a Pilot?

I used to beg my dad to drive to the airport to watch planes take-off and land at Pearson when I was a little kid. I would've spent all day there if I could. On family vacations, I would ask to meet the pilots on our flights, and would usually end up spending a fair amount of time in the cockpit, getting the pilots to show me the controls and systems. It must have left a lasting impression on me—I started my flight training at seventeen with the goal of becoming a professional pilot.

—Mike McDonald, B1900 Captain – SkyLink Express

I've always wanted to be a pilot, ever since I was a kid. Perhaps I was dropped on my head when I was a baby, I don't know.

—Shane Murphy, Corporate C550 Captain & Operations Manager

I decided to become a pilot for the simple love of flying! There was a moment flying commercially when I was little, when the 747 popped through the clouds and I think I knew instantly, right then.

—Heather Knox, Twin Otter First Officer—West Coast Air

I went for one flight in a Cessna 172 and I fell in love with flying.

—Susan Mileva, CRJ First Officer – Air Canada Jazz

I lived at the end of the local runway since I was five years old, and wanted to be a pilot ever since.

—Chris Prodaehl, King Air Captain – Fast Air

CHAPTER TWO: BEFORE STARTING OUT

When once you have tasted flight, you will forever walk the earth with your eyes turned skyward, for there you have been, and there you will always long to return.

—Leonardo da Vinci

T HE road to becoming a pilot in Canada is not an easy one. As I'll outline in the following chapters, choosing your path, getting your licences, and finding a job can be a long process. However, there are a few things you can do before pursuing your licences to make this journey easier. Even before you start flying, you should be evaluating whether or not it could be a career for you, as well as trying to meet people in the industry.

The Medical Exam

To be a pilot in Canada, not only do you have to possess a pilot licence, but you also have to pass a medical exam. In fact, your licence is not valid if you do not have a valid medical certificate with it. Flying can be a physically demanding experience. As a pilot, you're responsible for a very expensive plane and often numerous lives. Therefore, it's important that there are no possible safety hazards caused by potential health problems.

In Canada, there are four categories of medical certificates, as stated in the Canadian Aviation Regulations (CARS) 404.10:

1) A Category 1 medical certificate is required for the following licences:

> *(a)* commercial pilot licence—aeroplane or helicopter; and
>
> *(b)* airline transport pilot licence—aeroplane or helicopter.

(2) A Category 1 or 2 medical certificate is required for the following licences:

> *(a)* air traffic controller licence; and
>
> *(b)* flight engineer licence.

(3) A Category 1 or 3 medical certificate is required for the following permits, licences, and ratings:

> *(a)* student pilot permit—helicopter;
>
> *(b)* pilot permit—gyroplane;
>
> *(c)* private pilot licence—aeroplane or helicopter;
>
> *(d)* pilot licence—balloon;
>
> *(e)* flight instructor rating—glider; and
>
> *(f)* flight instructor rating—ultra-light aeroplane.

(4) A Category 1, 3, or 4 medical certificate is required for the following permits and licences:

> *(a)* student pilot permit—aeroplane;
>
> *(b)* pilot permit—recreational;
>
> *(c)* student pilot permit or pilot permit—ultra-light aeroplane;
>
> *(d)* student pilot permit—glider; and
>
> *(e)* pilot licence—glider.

As you can see, a Category 1 medical is required in order to receive a Commercial Pilot licence, although to start flying you only need a Category 4 medical—essentially a signed declaration form. All that is needed to obtain a private pilot licence is a Category 3 medical certificate. However, I'd recommend that you attempt to get a Category 1 medical from the start, to ensure that you're medically fit to one day obtain a commercial licence.

Each medical certificate has a different validity period:

Category 1: twelve months for holders under the age of forty, and six months for those over the age of forty. After those twelve months (six in the cases of pilots over the age of forty), the Category 1 medical reverts to a Category 3 medical. What this means is that while you can no longer practice the privileges of a commercial licence, you can still practice the privileges of a private licence. For example, if you are no longer flying as a career but still fly planes for fun, you can do so with a Category 3 medical.

Category 3: Sixty months for holders under forty and twenty-four months for those over forty.

Category 4: Sixty months depending on the student pilot rating held.

Outlining all the medical requirements to obtain a Category 1 medical certificate would take numerous pages of writing, along with a background in medicine or biology. If you would like to delve into the various requirements, or if you're having trouble sleeping and would like something dry to read, check out the Civil Aviation Medicine website at:

http://www.tc.gc.ca/CivilAviation/Cam/menu.htm.

I will discuss some of the more basic medical restrictions for obtaining a medical. Keep in mind that the Armed Forces and other various airlines will have different medical requirements in addition to the Category 1 medical certificate.

Vision: It is not necessary to have 20/20 vision to become a pilot. For a Category 1 medical certificate, it's necessary that vision can be corrected up to 20/30, while being no worse than 20/200 uncorrected. The refractive error must fall within the range of ± 3.0 diopters. If you require glasses to correct your vision up to 20/30, you are required to wear them while flying, and are required to have an extra set of corrective lenses with you while flying. Contact lenses are considered corrective eyewear, although a trial wear period of six months is necessary before this will be approved. It is not possible for someone who is significantly colour-blind to receive a Cat. 1 medical.

Hearing: Significant hearing loss will prevent a candidate from receiving a Cat. 1 medical. Candidates must demonstrate the ability to hear a whisper from six feet away in a quiet room. Candidates are also tested for hearing loss in different frequency ranges. The maximum allowable loss in either ear is 35 dB at 500, 1000, 2000 Hz and 50 dB at 3000 Hz.

General: There are numerous other medical requirements to obtain a Cat. 1 medical. Some of the more common limiting factors include:
    -Blood pressure out of the normal range
    -Alcohol or chemical dependency
    -Severe depression or being on anti-depressants
    -Psychological disorders

Any disease or disability with the potential to render the applicant unfit to safely operate an aircraft will make a candidate ineligible for a Cat. 1 medical. Having said that, many Canadian Aviation Examiners and the Civil Aviation Medicine branch of Transport Canada are prepared to work with potential candidates who are, for some reason, unable to pass the medical exam. They may explore the possibility of granting a medical certificate with limitations or restrictions to its holder. As an example, one restriction imposed may be a requirement for a pilot to fly with another crew member at all times.

To obtain a medical certificate, a candidate must go through a thorough medical exam. Candidates must also undergo an audiogram (a type of hearing test) at the initial exam, and at the first exam after age fifty-five. At the initial exam, candidates must also undergo an electrocardiogram, a test they will have to repeat once every two years after the age of thirty, and once every year after the age of forty. An electrocardiogram (ECG or EKG) measures the electric voltage of the heart and is used in screening for and diagnosing cardiovascular disease. This is accomplished by placing leads on different parts of the candidate's body and measuring the electrical potential between these leads.

On the Civil Aviation Website previously mentioned, you'll find a link that offers help in finding Canadian Aviation Medical Examiners. It's important to find an aviation doctor you trust and feel comfortable talking to.

While they are required to follow guidelines, a good relationship can make the difference between being able to keep your medical certificate and job, or having to find another line of work and hoping that you have illness insurance and a small mortgage. It's important to note that being nervous during an exam may increase your blood pressure above normal levels. One final note: try to abstain from sexual activity or excessive drinking for a few days, prior to your exam. Either of these could have an effect on the outcome of a medical exam.

Air Cadets

If you're sixteen or younger and think you might be interested in a career as a pilot, give serious thought to joining the Royal Canadian Air Cadets. Although I did not join the Air Cadets myself, I wish I had. I didn't find out about them until it was too late. Numerous friends and co-workers were in the Air Cadets during their teen years and really enjoyed the experience. Best of all, some of them received a glider licence and/or a private pilot licence free!

The Royal Canadian Air Cadets was founded during WWII and was initially created to provide a pool of trained pilots for the war effort. However, after the end of the war, its mandate changed to the following:

1. To develop, in youth, the attributes of good citizenship and leadership;
2. To promote physical fitness and a healthy lifestyle;
3. To stimulate an interest in the air element of the Canadian Forces.

In following this mandate, the Air Cadets have weekly meetings (parades), as well as some weekend excursions and annual summer camps—all free of charge.

Air Cadets is open to anyone between the ages of twelve and nineteen. However, if you join after the age of sixteen, it's difficult—though not impossible—to obtain a private pilot licence. This is because in deciding who will be one of the 320 cadets who attend the glider course and the 250 cadets who attend a power (airplane) course each summer, aptitude test scores as well as service to a cadet's particular squadron are taken into account. Therefore, the longer you've been in the program, the better chance you have of making a good impression and securing selection for the courses.

Besides offering the possibility of learning to fly, Air Cadets offers teenagers other opportunities such as foreign exchanges, developing leadership and public speaking skills, technical knowledge, and discipline. The weekly meetings usually involve drills, sports and games, first aid, and citizenship events that support the local community. Some squadrons even have a music program. Weekend excursions include visiting local Armed Forces Bases, visiting airports, sailing, camping, and marksmanship.

Air Cadets is not all fun and games, and is not for everyone. Military values are stressed, and they focus heavily on drills, discipline, and tidiness. For example, the uniform needs to be neatly pressed, and the boots need to be polished on a regular basis. Cadets are also expected to participate in volunteer public service activities, as well as some military ceremonies such as Remembrance Day. On the upside, many future employers recognize the commitment necessary to complete the program and look favourably on an applicant who has been a member of Air Cadets.

To join Air Cadets, contact your local squadron. Details can be found on the Cadets website:

http://www.cadets.ca/.

Keep in mind that this is the website for Air, Sea, and Army Cadets, so be sure to check that it's an Air Cadets squadron. Joining is free. The uniform that cadets are required to wear is loaned to the cadet from the Canadian Forces, and all that is asked in return is that good care be taken of the uniform. Parents and cadets are also encouraged to participate in fund-raising activities. When you join, you are *under no obligation* to join the regular or reserve armed forces afterwards—but if you are interested, the air cadet experience will likely give you a better idea of what to expect from military life. In the next chapter, I'll discuss one route to becoming a professional pilot: joining the military. Perhaps through the cadets program you'll find that it's a lifestyle you might enjoy.

The personal development opportunities are important aspects of Air Cadets, and the social development aspects will benefit you if you do decide to become a pilot. Many of my colleagues made some of their longest friendships in Air Cadets. As I'll discuss in Chapters 5 & 6, making connections is an important part of finding your first few jobs. Air Cadets offers a prime opportunity to meet people who will become future pilots. Not only will you get to know the cadets in your local squadron, but by attending summer camps, you'll get to meet cadets from all across the country—thus building your network of contacts in the industry. Numerous pilots that I've talked to have, at some point in their careers, found a job through a contact they made in Air Cadets.

Hangar Talk – Air Cadets

I did my private pilot's licence and glider's licence on a scholarship with the Air Cadets in Cornwall, Ontario.
—Geoff Cattrall, A340/A330 Second Officer – Cathay Pacific

I started out with the Air Cadet program and did my gliding and private pilots licence through them (Chilliwalk/Victoria respectively). The cadet courses were very structured, and anyone who went that route will tell you about the unique atmosphere of doing this kind of course in a six to seven week period with a great group of guys/gals. It was a blast! I would do it again any day. We were on top of our own little "Top Gun" worlds. I have no real complaints about the Cadet program, although the 'cadet' part of it takes some getting used to. It's a paramilitary structure, and there will always be a bed to clean, a uniform to iron, 'yes, sir,' 'no, sir,' 'three bags full, sir,' but looking back I'm sure I needed the discipline.
—Mike Stefanski, B1900D First Officer – Central Mountain Air

Intro Flights

Most people, especially those who live in larger cities, have been on a large airliner at least once in their life. This experience is quite different from being in a small single-engine trainer, or in a charter plane. Some people, while comfortable in a larger plane, feel very uncomfortable in a small plane. If you're thinking about training to become a pilot, it's imperative that you're comfortable in small planes—all your training and likely your first few jobs will be in these types of planes. Therefore, before you decide to become a pilot, I highly recommend going to your local flying school or club and taking an introductory or "fam" (familiarization) flight.

Intro flights range from $50-$100, and usually involve a ground briefing, followed by a thirty- or sixty-minute flight with an instructor. The ground briefing will usually go over the basic controls of the aircraft, where the flight will go, and what all the instruments are for. The instructor will then demonstrate a "walk-around," explaining the different parts of the aircraft and how each part can affect flight. After the walk-around is finished, you'll be buckled up in the plane for the flight. The flight instructor will likely give you a quick safety briefing, as well as a more detailed description of the controls. After the "run-up," which is essentially warming up and checking the engine, you'll taxi to the runway for your flight (don't be alarmed if your instructor fails to perform a run-up or walk-around—it's possible they were flying the same plane right before your flight). For most introductory flights, your fight instructor will usually perform the take-off while demonstrating how to control the plane. Once a safe altitude is reached, the instructor will perform a few basic manoeuvres such as climbs, descents, and turns, and then let you fly the plane yourself. Don't worry, the pilot will have another set of controls and will not let you do anything dangerous.

The flight will be over before you know it. Don't be discouraged if you found it a little unnerving, or even felt a little air sick. If you've never been in a small plane before, it can take some getting used to. Not only are you much closer to the doors and windows (in some small planes you can just open the window to cool things down if you want!), but you can also feel even the lightest turbulence in the air. Even the most experienced pilots feel a little queasy on occasion. Now, if you found it terrifying and could not wait for the flight to end, flying might not be for you. Slight discomfort and nerves are to be expected at first, but you'll soon get used to things after a few flights.

After your flight, you will get a debriefing from your instructor. While most instructors and schools will not pressure you to book more lessons, keep in mind that an introductory flight is essentially an advertisement or a test drive. They want you sign up and take all future flying lessons there, but do not feel obligated to commit to this. In fact, I recommend going to other nearby flight schools and taking additional introductory flights. Not only can you get the feel for each school, but you can also log hours towards your licences at an often-discounted price.

A Back-up Plan

I had a tough time deciding where in the book to place this section. I've decided to put it near the beginning, since I feel it's a very important thing to consider when choosing how to best pursue a flying career. Except for professional athletes, there are very few professions that are as dependent upon good health as flying. As mentioned above, you need to undergo frequent medical examinations, and the job itself can be tough on the body. Part of a pilot's life involves flying at odd night time hours, getting up early one day and staying up late the next, and airline pilots routinely jump back and forth between time zones.

The industry itself can also be volatile. Airlines are constantly emerging and going out of business. As can be seen with some of the traditional legacy carriers in the US after Sept. 11th, even a pilot with thirty years on the job is not immune. Canada has had a number of smaller airlines come and go. The industry is very susceptible to economic recession. When the economy is slow and people need to watch their spending, one of the first expenses they cut is vacationing. Instead of flying somewhere, they might decide on camping instead.

On top of general economic concerns, entry-level jobs are often only seasonal. Many smaller operators do the vast majority of their flying during the heavy tourist seasons in the summer. With very little traffic in the winter, some smaller airlines and charter outfits will routinely lay off staff during that time.

A future concern is the trend of rising oil prices. Because of the world's dependence on oil and the ever-dwindling oil supplies, the oil that does remain is often more expensive to obtain. As a result, some environmentalists and economists are predicting that the price of oil will continue to increase dramatically. This will play a significant role in the airline industry. Higher ticket prices could lead to a decrease in the demand for air travel.

These thoughts are not meant to scare you away from aviation, but rather to explain the background for creating a back up plan. After I'd been flying Medevacs for a year, I started having some minor health problems. They were not significant enough for me to lose my medical certificate or endanger the safety of my passengers, but they were enough to make flying a lot less enjoyable. This, along with the desire to continue my education, is what prompted me to return to school. While I am not suggesting that everyone should follow the exact same path as me, I am suggesting that every potential future pilot think about what they would do if they suddenly lost their medical certificate or were laid off. How would you pay your bills? Do you have any skills for another job that you would enjoy?

Every pilot should have a back up plan in place, in case flying fails to work out. This plan will be different for everyone. Some opt for a trade or a more labour-intensive job; some try to branch out to other jobs in the aviation industry; some continue with their education. One of the perquisites of a flying job is that you often have a fair number of days off. On their days off, pilots may focus on a trade, or work in construction or landscaping. While not everybody's cup of tea, these jobs can offer good pay and flexible hours. Each trade has varying amounts of educational and apprenticing requirements. Some simply require on-the-job training, where others require some in-class-instruction. For more information, go to http://www.apprenticetrades.ca/.

Obtaining a university degree is not essential for becoming a pilot, but as will be discussed in Chapter 9, it can increase your chances of being hired by a major airline. Aviation aside, a degree will open up many other opportunities. A bachelor's degree is a requirement for many non-aviation jobs—companies may not even consider you for a position without it. Earning a degree will also open the door into graduate degree programs, and professional programs in fields such as medicine, law, and education. An aviation background combined with any sort of professional training will make you even more marketable in a wide range of fields.

Within any airline, there are a number of opportunities to diversify your experience. Some airlines offer an aircraft maintenance engineer (AME) apprentice program. A degree can also make you eligible for management positions within airlines, particularly if the degree is in a business-related field. Adding a degree to your aviation experience may allow you to be considered for positions in the areas of training, human resources, or marketing.

It's possible to obtain a degree completely through distance education. In Canada, Athabasca University (http://www.athab ascau.ca/) and The University of Waterloo (http://www.uwater loo.ca/) have the most developed distance education programs, but there are many universities that offer similar programs. The cost of a single course is around $500 for a half-year course. Thirty to forty courses are required to complete a bachelor's degree, depending on your chosen subject. Universities are designing more and more courses that can be completed entirely over the Internet. Some courses are completed through correspondence, whereas others can be completed mostly via distance education; certain courses will require a class exam or a practical evaluation. Some universities may offer prior credit for a college diploma or previous work experience. In the US, Embry Riddle Aeronautical University (http://www.em bryriddle.edu/) offers distance education courses that focus on aviation. Although the courses are quite expensive (approximately $800 per course), an Embry Riddle degree is internationally recognized and is well respected in the aviation industry. However, there is no guarantee that such a degree will help you get your first flying job.

The opportunities really are endless. With the Internet and today's computer technology, it's possible to run a business or con-tinue your education from almost anywhere in the world. There's no specific path to securing a good back up plan, but it is something that I think is extremely important. In aviation, so much of your training focuses on what to do if something goes wrong—shouldn't it be the same with your career?

Women in Aviation

Aviation has traditionally been a male-dominated industry. The stereotypical airline pilot has generally been a white, middle-aged male. The truth is, pilots come in all shapes and sizes. Of the 47,000+ licensed airplane pilots in Canada today, approximately 2,800 are women. Although this is still a relatively low percentage, it's increasing all the time. With the social changes that have occurred over the past few decades, Canadian women face the challenge of having to juggle a career and family. Even for regular jobs, this can be a challenging task. If children are young, schedules must be flexible so parents can meet their needs. For a regular office job, it's tricky if your child is sick at school, as you will often have to take the afternoon off to come pick them up. This is even more complicated for pilots. You cannot divert an airliner because your child threw up at school! Although this type of challenge does affect men, it continues to affect women more.

Another challenge women face is the old-school, chauvinistic attitude that views flying as job reserved only for men In the past, some of the smaller operators have been known to avoid hiring female pilots, and it can sometimes be more difficult for women to gain first jobs with small northern operators. Thankfully, this attitude is disappearing. It's now more common to see female pilots, and many female colleagues I've spoken to have reassured me that their gender has not limited their ability to be successful in their career, and that they haven't experienced discrimination. In fact, with many larger airlines attempting to diversify and show that they are, in fact, equal opportunity employers, being female may actually increase your chances of being hired. Unfortunately, this can lead some people to believe that women are being hired as pilots simply because they are women, regardless of qualifications. This is not to say that female pilots are being hired ahead of men who possess considerably more experience, but all things being equal, an airline may be more inclined to choose a female candidate over a male. The reality of the situation is that today, airlines will not attempt to hire anyone—male or female—who is unfit for a job. Although it can be frustrating to be told you were hired simply because you're a female pilot, the truth is that you deserve, and are qualified for the position. Any detractors are simply jealous.

A number of associations promote women in aviation. The two major groups are the Ninety-Nines and Women in Aviation. The Ninety-Nines formed in 1929 as an organization that provided "good fellowship, jobs, and a central office and files on women in aviation." The name was proposed by Amelia Earhart and is based on the initial Ninety-Nine charter members of the group. Today, the organization has over 5,500 members, and has the following for its mission statement:

Promote: World fellowship through flight

Provide: Networking and scholarship opportunities
                for women and aviation education in the
                community

Preserve: The unique history of women in aviation

The Ninety-Nines offer some networking opportunities and operate a museum of women's accomplishments in aviation. Their websites can be found at:

http://www.ninety-nines.org/
http://www.canadian99s.org/

Women in Aviation is a non-profit organization dedicated to the encouragement and advancement of women in all aviation career fields and interests. Although similar to the Ninety-Nines, Women in Aviation focuses more on networking, education, and employment resources for women pilots. Women in Aviation also actively promotes aviation as a career for women. The websites can be found at:

http://www.wai.org/
http://www.cwia.ca/

As well as providing support, resources, and networking opportunities, both of these organizations provide scholarships for female flight students. Flight training can be expensive, and if you are a female looking to get your pilot licence, I would highly recommend looking into both of these groups. From talking with some of my female colleagues, the consensus is that, despite being treated well by male colleagues, participation in these groups provides a refreshing break from a male dominated workplace, and an opportunity to socialize with other female pilots—all of whom understand the unique challenges that women face in the aviation industry.

Hangar Talk – Women in Aviation

Don't be swayed by the frightening numbers of men in this industry. Women pilots are just as capable as their male counterparts. Just make sure that you don't have a problem spending hour upon hour with a group of guys—because trust me, you're about to.
—Heather Knox, Twin Otter First Officer – West Coast Air

People in general, and male pilots in particular, sometimes automatically assume you're a bad pilot until you prove them wrong. So getting a job is quite challenging considering most Chief Pilots are male. Things are slowly getting better, though, and now women get that chance to prove themselves almost on equal basis as men (mostly in the bigger companies). Realize that flying is not all glory, fun, and partying. You'll also have to work hard, learn a lot, and prove yourself to many people! But if you really got into it for the right reason (which is the love of flying), and when you are flying for the airline of your dreams, you will realize that it IS the best job in the world, and you will have a smile on your face every time you go to work (even if it is at 5:00 AM).
—Susan Mileva, CRJ First Officer – Air Canada Jazz

Feminism and women's rights are a relatively new concept. Women have come a long way in the last 100 years, and changing a society's mentality is not an easy feat. I think we will see a lot more female pilots in the next few decades.
—Darlene Sly, Twin Otter First Officer – Winward Island Airways

CHAPTER THREE: HOW TO GET YOUR LICENCE

I'm learning to fly, but I ain't got wings
Coming down is the hardest thing

—Tom Petty, 'Learning to Fly'

U NLIKE other professions such as law, medicine, or education, where you have to go to law school, medical school, or teacher's college, there is not one specific route to obtain pilot qualifications. Traditionally, pilots have obtained their licences either through private local flight schools or through the military. More recently, college and university aviation programs have become more prominent in the training of pilots. Each of these routes offers different advantages and disadvantages for the aspiring pilot. Different people in the industry will have their own ideas as to which route is best. My own opinion is that there is no single best way—just the correct route for each particular individual. Before choosing a route, it's important to think about your goals as a pilot and your unique situation. What type of job do you ultimately want? What type of education are you hoping to get? Where do you want to work? Do you want flexibility in your training, or do you prefer following a set schedule? Are you hoping to stay close to home, or do you want to travel to a different part of the country?

Flight Schools

Local flight schools have long been the dominant form of flight training in Canada.

Most cities will have a school or two at the local airport. These schools will operate as training facilities and a place from which planes can be rented. Some flight schools may have a small charter operation to compliment their flight training services. Training at a flight school usually takes two forms: ground school and flight training. Depending on demand, ground school courses are usually held one or two nights each week over the period of a few months, varying by school. Private pilot ground school, of which forty-five hours is required for a private licence, covers topics that include basic airmanship, navigation, meteorology, and technical knowledge. At a flight school, you will usually deal with a single instructor who will be responsible for your in-flight training, and it's very likely that this will be a different person than your ground school instructor. He or she will follow a basic syllabus outlined by Transport Canada to cover all the required lesson plans. Each lesson will generally consist of pre-flight and post-flight briefings, as well as an actual flight.

There are many benefits to training at a traditional flight school, the most important being flexibility. Flight schools are a business, and you're their customer. As a result, they are more apt to cater to your needs. Unlike a college, where classes are taught at specific times, flight schools will offer you a choice of class and flight times. Although ground school courses are often on a set schedule, they're usually at times outside normal working hours—enabling you to attend even if you have a full-time job. This can make paying for your flight training considerably easier. If you're able to work full-time and pay-as-you-go for your flight training, you'll be able to avoid the heavy debt and student loans many pilots are left with post flight school.

At most flight schools, you can set your own pace. You do not have this luxury with most college aviation programs, which for the most part will dictate when your vacations will be and when you'll start and finish your training.

There are, however, some downsides to completing your flight training at a traditional flight school. These can include cost, lack of discipline, lack of contacts, and possibly less extensive ground-school training.

The expensive nature of training at a traditional flight school is often mitigated by the flexibility they offer, but it should be noted that many of these schools are ineligible for student loans. Therefore, all training expenses would need to be subsidized by savings, or financed through a bank. While training at a traditional flight school offers the potential to finish your licences more quickly, your training may have to be postponed if your funds run low. This may or may not be advantageous for some students, depending on your financial situation.

The flexibility of training at a flight school may be beneficial for some, but can be detrimental to others. For some people, a program that instils discipline and requires students to adhere to strict deadlines is just what is needed. While training at a flight school, you are your own boss, and therefore set your own schedule. This freedom can be wonderful, but it should never be forgotten that this freedom comes with responsibility—if you've had a bad week, will you have the necessary motivation to get yourself going? For some people, it might be easy to slip behind in your training, thus prolonging the time it takes to earn your qualifications.

Traditional flight schools often offer less of an opportunity for networking when compared to their college counterparts. Depending on the size of your flight school, it's very possible that you will meet few, if any, other people besides your instructor. In flight school, you complete your training at your own pace, and the majority of your lessons will be with your regular instructor—compare this to flight college, where you'll have many classmates and a series of in- structors. This is not to say that opportunities for networking do not exist in a traditional flight school, but it may prove more difficult than with other programs. As you'll see in subsequent chapters, networking is an extremely important factor in finding a job.

Another potential downside to training at a traditional flight school as opposed to aviation college, is the less formal training you'll receive, and also the likelihood that you will experience far less immersion in the subject of aviation. Again, I'm not saying that flight schools provide inadequate training, only that colleges generally tend to provide more extensive backgrounds on many aviation topics. Ground-training at flight schools typically run one or two nights a week, whereas classes at colleges take place every day, and often for longer hours. It's simply easier to cover more material in a college environment. In this setting, you may have a better opportunity to absorb more material as you and your classmates become immersed in the college aviation experience. I've also heard many arguments that the material covered in numerous college aviation courses is superfluous and often not applicable to everyday situations. I'll be the first to admit that I've forgotten most of the specifics of the various thermodynamics and statics courses that I took in college, but some of the basic concepts have been helpful.

Hangar Talk – Flight Schools

I did my private and commercial training at a Flying Club in British Columbia. Overall, I really enjoyed the friendly club atmosphere. However, as a general criticism of Flight Schools, many of the instructors have no commercial experience, and therefore don't really know what it's like to work in aviation outside of the training environment.

—Angus Forsyth, CL215 First Officer, C310 Captain

I did all my training at a Flying Club in Ontario. I liked that it was close to home, but didn't like that a lot of the equipment was pretty old.

—Andy Gould, Metro Medevac First Officer—Perimeter Airlines

My flight training was at Centennial Aviation for my Private & Commercial, and Pro IFR for my Multi-IFR. Location, location, location! Both were close to home. Pro IFR had excellent service, training, and equipment. At the time when I was training, both Centennial and Pro IFR were very busy. Sometimes it was hard to book a plane. It actually delayed the completion of my multi-IFR by six months.

—Matt Hogan, Airbus A320 First Officer

Don't keep all your money in one basket; pay as you fly. Don't leave lump sums of money in the training school bank account because as in my case, you don't get it back if the company goes bankrupt. Concentrate and dedicate yourself and fly as much as you can, because the less you fly, the more likely you will forget things, and that'll cost you more money and time. The faster you're done

achieving your licence/ratings/building hours, the sooner you will land your first job.
  —*Altaf Rashid, B1900D Captain—Falcon Express Cargo Airlines, Dubai, United Arab Emirates*

Colleges

The newest trend in flight training has been the advent of College Aviation Programs. Each program is unique. Academically, some focus on the more technical aspects of aviation, some focus on business and management, and some provide a general arts education coupled with a flight training component. For the in-flight component, some colleges operate their own fleet of aircraft, while others have an agreement with a local flight training school that provides the flight training. Some flight schools simply develop a non-affiliated "commercial pilot diploma" program (see pilot diploma section). The industry focus for each of these programs also differs. Some focus on providing training for an eventual career with an airline, while others focus on float flying and bush pilot instruction. The costs of these programs can vary greatly. Some are extremely expensive because of the high costs of post-secondary education and the high costs of flight training. Other programs are roughly equivalent in price to flight training at a local flight school. A small number in Ontario are subsidized, and are therefore far less expensive than the average flight training program.

Each college has its own admissions criteria. Generally, some high school credit in math, physics, and science courses is required. Some programs also require an entrance exam or interview. The subsidized colleges in Ontario (Sault College, Confederation College, and Seneca College) are all over-enrolled programs; not all who apply will be accepted. Some other non-subsidized colleges are also over-enrolled, while others will accept all candidates who meet the minimum requirements. Following your acceptance, some colleges have extremely high standards that you must meet. These standards are often measured in post-acceptance examinations that you must pass in order to remain in the program. Other, less-stringent colleges, allow their students to continue re-taking the exams until they pass.

Similar to regular flight schools, the location of a particular college is also an important factor in your decision-making. Some colleges are located close to urban areas with busy airspace and airports, whereas others are located in remote towns. This can be either beneficial or detrimental to the student, depending on his or her circumstances. There are wide varieties of choices when selecting a college.

There are many benefits to completing your flight training through an accredited college. To begin with, colleges sometimes offer more extensive ground-school courses than traditional flight schools. This is particularly the case in the technical and theoretical aspects of aviation, such as aircraft design, mechanics, electricity, and meteorology. While often impractical, an in-depth knowledge of background information is not only valuable for some airline technical interviews, but can also make new concepts and information easier to digest. For example, the aerodynamics and physics used in aircraft design are extremely complex, and while you do not need to fully understand this information to pilot an aircraft, a basic understanding of the information is invaluable. Many colleges offer aviation focused business courses, a background in business, which will give you a better understanding of the aviation industry. While an understanding of supply and demand will not make you a better pilot, it may make you a more valuable employee.

Another benefit of college training, when compared to flight school training, is that a college will enforce discipline, and has a pre-determined training schedule that each student must follow. For some, this stringent schedule may be a reason not to attend a college. However, having a program that must be followed provides an added incentive to get the extra studying done. Some colleges even require you to follow a certain dress code when flying and attending classes. If you're the type of person who can't stand being told what to wear, this may not sound like a great idea. On the other hand, you could consider it a rehearsal for a time when you're qualified and flying commercially, because almost any job you land in the aviation industry will require you to wear a uniform or follow a dress code. Would you pass up a job at Air Canada just because you don't want to wear their uniform? Appearances are important! Can you imagine if you were sitting at an airport waiting to board a flight and a person with dirty and ripped clothes, scruffy hair, and flip-flops announced they were going to be your pilot? Would you want to get on that plane?

College aviation programs are based at provincially accredited colleges and universities, and therefore increase the likelihood of your securing government loans. Most banks also offer a student line of credit that's accessible to students enrolled in an accredited college or university. Be sure to check into both your provincial student aid program and your bank for their potential forms of funding. In this respect, you may also enjoy some of the privileges associated with attending a college or university, such as student discounts, gym memberships, and health and dental insurance. The subsidized colleges (Sault College, Confederation College, and Seneca College) offer flight training at extremely discounted rates. Students pay regular college tuition, along with some ancillary fees, and all the flight training is included. The existence of such subsidized programs is often a topic of controversy, especially during down times in the industry, where finding an entry-level job is extremely difficult. But if money is a factor and you're an Ontario resident, I would strongly recommend looking into a subsidized program. Generally, in the subsidized colleges, the academics tend to be more competitive with a greater chance of being kicked out than in other courses. However, the financial rewards alone could be worth it if you're successful.

The social aspect of college programs should not be overlooked. It offers you the opportunity to mingle with fellow students, all of whom share your interest in aviation. Studying with your fellow students will also greatly benefit your learning, and by the time you graduate, you'll have an entire host of contacts in the industry. As you progress in your career, these contacts formed during your college years will allow you to learn about job postings through word-of-mouth and personal recommendations.

Despite what some colleges or programs will tell you (this is more so in the US than in Canada), going to a particular college will not guarantee you a job. However, it may help you at the airline level, since Air Canada and other international airlines look favourably on an aviation college diploma or a university degree. At the entry level, though, having a diploma will likely not help you obtain employment. In my opinion, aviation college programs often focus too much on training students for a career with an airline, and focus too little on training for a first job. Fancy jet simulators are fun toys, but they will not help you get a first job on a small bush plane. Although there is one operator that is based in Norman Wells, NWT that will only hire candidates with an aviation college diploma, most entry-level airlines do not really care about where you did your training. Depending on where the Chief Pilot did his or her training, you may have a leg up on the competition if you happen to have gone to the same college as him or her. However, it's inadvisable to choose a college based on where a certain Chief Pilot attended. In fact, some of the more bush-type operators have a bias against college graduates. I've even heard one Chief Pilot claim that he would never hire a graduate from a particular college. (But according to his colleagues, he tends to be stubborn and not well liked; so maybe never having the opportunity to fly with him is a blessing in disguise). The college you attend can certainly play a part in determining which jobs you get, but other factors, such as how hard you work and who you know, are of far more importance.

One final advantage to attending an Aviation College is that in the Spring of 2007, Air Canada Jazz quietly announced that it would be experimenting with a pilot project that would take the top three graduates from select colleges and give them an opportunity to interview for a direct entry First Officer position. This would be an incredible opportunity for pilots interested in a career with a regional and eventually major airline. At the time of printing however, the program has yet to come to fruition and it remains to be seen how successful such a program will be, how many graduates will success-fully complete the company training and whether the program will be repeated in subsequent years. There may also be issues with integrating these college graduates with the rest of the pilots as numerous current pilots have expressed their displeasure with the idea. Regardless, this would be an amazing opportunity for a newly licenced college graduate and when deciding whether to attend college and which one you will attend, it would be wise to inquire about the status of this program.

Although there are a number of advantages to attending a col-lege aviation program, college is not for everyone. College programs tend to be less flexible than local flight schools. This is especially so if the college operates their fleet in-house. On top of a full schedule of classes, your flights are often scheduled for you, giving you very little flexibility in your schedule. While this may provide practice for when you're working as a pilot in the real world by following someone else's schedule, it can be impractical when you are trying to work to pay for school.

College programs will generally have specific start and finish dates and a have a set duration. This means you must complete your flight training at the pace chosen by your college—even if you wanted to get your licence more quickly, you would not be able to. Although there were a few older students when I went through my college program, most programs tend to focus on younger students who have just finished high school or a university degree program. It would likely prove difficult for someone with work and family commitments to contend with the demanding schedule of some college aviation programs. That is not to say that it's impossible, but in this situation, it may make more sense to utilize the flexibility offered from a traditional flight school. The training regime in college is also much less flexible than with a traditional flight school. You may not be able to choose your in-flight instructors, and your cross-country flights can sometimes be limited to a few approved destinations.

Not all college programs are created equal. Of the colleges discussed in the upcoming list, many have a long history and are recognized throughout the industry. A few remain unfamiliar even to me. Some programs have had a shady past (particularly joint college/flight school ventures), with some even going out of business, resulting in the loss of significant amounts of money for their students, and, frustratingly, delaying their students' training. When choosing a college, talk to people other than your parents and the school. Try to talk to pilots in the industry and to companies where you would eventually like to work, both for entry-level positions and for airline-type jobs. This will give you a better understanding of the industry's attitude regarding a particular program.

A Cessna 172 from Coastal Pacific
photo by Mike Stefanski

Hangar Talk – Flight College

I did my training at a College. I really liked the structure surrounding the program…very regimented. I also liked the college atmosphere and could concentrate on schooling alone (no work or university on the side). A disadvantage of some colleges is that training can take three years or more and could probably be done quicker through a private flight school.

—*Gerry Robinson, Metro Captain – Bearskin Airlines*

I graduated from Seneca College. I liked the fact that Seneca had good equipment and that the program was structured, even though it took longer to complete my training than at a private flight school. I would take the same route again, and I feel the Seneca name is recognized and the connections to be made are plentiful.

—*Colin Reeson, Piaggio Avanti Captain – FlightExec*

Looking back, I don't regret taking the college route. It was enjoyable and is great for establishing an initial base of contacts within the industry. However, if I had to do it over again, I would have concentrated on getting my PPL/CPL and Instructor Rating on my own time—i.e., got it done faster- (within a year). Then I would have enrolled for an undergraduate degree and worked part-time as a flight instructor, while conducting university studies. (expensive process though!)

—Mike McDonald, B1900 Captain – Skylink Express

I went to Selkirk College in Castlegar, BC. I liked the fact that we got great mountain flying experience, unlimited use of the simulator, and had a well-structured program. I didn't like the fact that Castlegar didn't have an ILS, and we weren't able to do night flying there so we had to fly to other airports to get that experience.

—Greg McMaster, Convair CV 580 First Officer – Conair

List Of Aviation College Programs

College—Own Fleet

CEGEP Chicoutimi – Chicoutimi, PQ
✈ 3 years – Aviation Diploma CEGEP
✈ http://www.cegep-chicoutimi.qc.ca/cqfa/
✈ All courses conducted in French – Quebec government CEGEP program

Confederation College – Thunder Bay, ON
✈ 2.5 years – Aviation Flight Management Diploma
✈ http://www.confederationc.on.ca/ace/
✈ Float training offered instead of multi-engine training
✈ Subsidized

Moncton Flight College – Moncton, NB
✈ 20 months – Diploma of Aviation Technology
✈ http://www.mfc.nb.ca/

Mount Royal College – Calgary, AB
✈ 2 years – Aviation Diploma
✈ http://business.mtroyal.ca/aviation/index.shtml
✈ students must complete their private pilot licence prior to starting

Sault College – Sault Ste. Marie, ON
✈ 3 year – Diploma of Aviation Technology

✈ http://www.saultcollege.ca/Aviation/default.htm
✈ Subsidized

Selkirk College – Castlegar, BC
✈ 2 years – Professional Aviation Diploma
✈ http://selkirk.ca/programs/ba/Aviation/

Seneca College – Toronto, ON
✈ 4 years – Bachelor of Applied Technology (Applied Degree Program)
✈ http://aviation.senecac.on.ca/
✈ Co-op program—Subsidized

College Program in Conjunction with a Private Flight School

The following list includes the college, the length of the program, the corresponding flight school, and the website address:

Territories

Aurora College – Yellowknife, NWT
✈ 1.5 years
✈ Big River Air Ltd.
✈ http://www.auroracollege.nt.ca/

British Columbia

BCIT – Vancouver, BC
✈ 64 weeks
✈ Pacific Flying Club
✈ http://www.bcit.ca/study/programs/1055dipts

Okanagan College
✈ 2 years
✈ Carson Air
✈ http://www.okanagan.bc.ca/page630.aspx

UFCV /Coastal Pacific – Abbottsford, BC
✈ 1, 2, or 4 years

✈ Coastal Pacific Aviation
✈ http://coastalpacific.com/cpa/index.html

Alberta

Bow Valley – Calgary, AB
✈ 18 to 24 months
✈ Calgary Flight Centre
✈ http://www.calgaryflight.com/Training%20Centre/DiplomaPrograme.htm

Grant MacEwan College – Edmonton, AB
✈ 1 or 2 years
✈ Cooking Lake Aviation Academy
✈ http://business.macewan.ca/gmcc/management/Program/DetailsPage.cfm?id=1100

Medicine Hat College – Medicine Hat, AB
✈ 2 years
✈ Bar XH Aviation
✈ http://www.mhc.ab.ca/calendar/programs/info.php?program=10

Northern Alberta IT
✈ 2 years
✈ Centennial Flight Centre
✈ http://www.nait.ca/programs/AVT/

Red Deer College – Red Deer, AB
✈ 2 years
✈ Sky Wings Aviation Academy
✈ http://www.rdc.ab.ca/programs_and_courses/other_training_opportunities/aviation.html

Saskatchewan

Saskatchewan Institute of Applied Science and Technology
✈ 1 year

✈ Done in conjunction with any flying school; students must have their private licence before enrolling
✈ http://www.siast.sk.ca/siast/educationtraining/oncampusprogra ms/7260/6031/5850/index.shtml#programoverview

Manitoba

Red River College – Winnipeg, MB
✈ 2 years
✈ Harv's Air & Winnipeg Aviation
✈ http://me.rrc.mb.ca/Catalogue/ProgramFrame.asp?ProgCode= AQT

Ontario

Algonquin College – Ottawa, ON
✈ 1 year
✈ Ottawa Flying Club
✈ http://www.algonquincollege.com/sat/aviation/

Canadore College – North Bay, ON – Aboriginal program
✈ 3 years
✈ First Nations Technical Institute – Aviation
✈ http://www.canadorec.on.ca/Programs/FullTime/Aviation/AV FWA01.cfm

Conestoga – Kitchener, ON
✈ 2 years
✈ Waterloo-Wellington Flight Centre
✈ http://www.conestogac.on.ca/jsp/programs/schoolliberalmedia /liberal/gaspaviation.jsp

Georgian College – Barrie, ON
✈ 3 years
✈ http://www.georgianc.on.ca/aviation/about.htm

Lambton College – Sarnia, ON
✈ 1 year
✈ Huron Flight Centre

✈ http://www.lambton.on.ca//Programs/program_html?PROGC
ODE=A596&LASTRECORDID=1879

Quebec

Institut Grasset—Montreal, PQ
✈ 1.5 years
✈ Académie de l'Aviation
✈ http://www.institut-grasset.qc.ca/html/p_p_pilotage.html

University Degree Programs

University of Western Ontario – London, ON
✈ 4 years
✈ Empire Aviation
✈ http://deansoffice.ssc.uwo.ca/acs/aviation/

University of New Brunswick – Fredricton, NB
✈ Capital Airways
✈ 3 years – Bachelor of Business Administration
✈ http://extend.unb.ca/aviation/

UCFV * (degree program available) – Abbotsford, BC
✈ Coastal Pacific Aviation

Pilot Diploma Programs

Some traditional flight schools have attempted to compete with college aviation programs by creating professional or commercial pilot diploma programs. I've not included these in the list of colleges for two reasons. First, they're difficult to list, often emerging and disappearing with demand; second, I'm not convinced about their merit.

Flight schools will create a diploma program by adding a number of classroom courses to their regular flight training program. The increased number of courses can include more extensive meteorology, maintenance, and business school classes. Some of these courses can be specifically tailored to an individual area, or to a specific type of flying.

Please realize, I'm not knocking the quality of training you may be receiving if you're already enrolled in one of these programs. That said, I'm not sure if I see the advantages of these programs when compared to traditional flight training or an accredited college program. You have the downside of higher commitment and less flexibility than traditional flight training, without the benefits of an accredited college diploma. Despite being a proponent of more education to aid in students' decision-making, obtaining this information via an accredited collage, rather than from a traditional flight school, may have added benefits. If you went to Bill & Ted's flight school's professional pilot diploma program, you may have had training from the world's best two instructors, but since the program is unknown and not recognized, it may fail to offer you any hard advantages when applying for a job. While you may still have some soft advantages (networking, for example), without accreditation or recognition, your diploma may not help you in the job hunt.

Having the program administered through a traditional flight school, rather than an accredited college, could cause eligibility difficulties when attempting to receive government student loans and other types of funding. At traditional schools, you have the flexibility to plan your flight training around your job, but with a professional pilot program you may not have that flexibility. Everybody's different, and who knows—there may be a diploma program put on through a traditional flight school that's perfect for you. Just do your homework prior to deciding on your diploma program—they're not all created equal.

The Armed Forces

Military Aviation in Canada has a long and proud tradition. In World War II, The British Commonwealth Air Training Plan facilitated the building of numerous airports across the country, a number of which still exist today. Canada's vast space and distance from the main theatres of combat made it a perfect place to train the Allied Forces' pilots. After WWII, Canada played an important role as a NATO ally in the Cold War. Today, Canada's military role in the world is changing to include humanitarian missions for both the UN and NATO, and security roles in the "war on terror." As a result, the role of military aviation in Canada is constantly changing.

A career in the military is not for everyone. Serving one's country is a unique way of life that requires numerous sacrifices. Flight training in the military is unlike flight training at a flight school or college; after training at a college or flight school, your final certification is in the form of a commercial pilot licence, whereas in the military, your final certification is under the military banner. The type of flights you perform, as well as the type of training you receive, is military specific. With military training, you're trained to be a military aviator, which involves training to be a pilot as well as training to be a military officer.

Military training is more structured and formalized than civilian flight training. For example, pilots who are military-trained undergo extensive non-flight specific training, such as Basic Officer Training and second language training. Acceptance to military pilot training is a long and challenging process, but the potential rewards are great. Military pilots are military officers. As a result, a four-year bachelor degree is required either prior to or subsequent to joining. If you're still in high school and are considering a career in the military, Royal Military College may be a good option for your university education. RMC offers a wide selection of undergraduate degrees, combined with military training paid for by the Canadian Forces (in return for a designated number of years service in the Forces). After completion of their university program, pilot candidates attend wings training and then aircraft-specific training. Pilot candidates with a university education can also join the military with the direct entry program, which, depending on the Air Force's need, sometimes includes students or graduates of college aviation programs. The military also has stricter medical requirements than that of a civilian class 1 medical. For example, the military requires uncorrected 20/20 vision (although this may be changing in the near future) and has weight and height restrictions depending upon the type of aircraft flown. For example, for the CF-18 Hornet, you have to be under a certain weight and height in order for the ejection seat to function properly. Definitely important!

The process involved in becoming a Canadian Armed Forces pilot includes the following:

+ applying/testing
+ Basic Officer Training
+ second language training
+ initial wings flight training
+ type-specific flight training (jets, multi-engine, helicopters)
+ aircraft-specific training
+ service

After enrolling in the military under the above pilot stream, you are required, at a minimum, to commit to five years of service directly following the receipt of your wings. It can often take years to receive your wings, though, since you must first complete other forms of training (Basic Officer Training and second-language training). All this training is in addition to having a degree! This is a big commitment. According to the military, it costs more than $2 million to train a single pilot, and they expect a return on their investment. It would not be to their benefit to train a pilot and then have him or her immediately leave for the airlines. Therefore, the decision to join the military is not to be made lightly.

There are a number of benefits to flying for the military. To begin with, the types of flights and missions are vastly different than with a civilian job. Flying almost any type of military aircraft is likely more exciting than flying an airliner. Depending on the type of aircraft, flights can involve formation flying, low-level navigation, aerobatic manoeuvres, and super-sonic speeds. You'll not experience any of this flying for an airline, where even the slightest bit of turbulence can upset some of the more timid passengers. Deployment into an area of conflict, while not high on most people's list of dream jobs, would no doubt be exciting. Military flying can also be very diverse. Initially, you'll be posted to an aircraft based partially on your requests, but mostly on operational need. However, after a certain number of years, again based on operational need, you can request a transfer to a different posting. For example, you might fly a C-130 Hercules for a few years and then get transferred to a helicopter, or onto a jet. The Air Force is also the only place where you can do some types of flying, such as flying fighter jets.

Flying in the military also offers more job security than civilian flying. Although some potential pilots may be put off by the military's mandatory five-year commitment, you are guaranteed income during those five years. It's not necessary to hunt for your next job if you get laid off, and you eliminate the risk of the airline you work for going under. For the most part, the military operates outside the market. Even if you become medically unfit to fly, you can be positioned elsewhere in the forces, since your training has encompassed both flying and non-flying job skills.

There are a few problems with a career in the military. First, it's a long road to become a pilot. Even more so than with the college route, someone else will dictate your training schedule to you. This is also the case when you've completed your training. Second, your life is essentially not your own throughout your time in the military, and many decisions are made for you.

One of the main reasons I decided against a career in the military, besides the long commitment, is that as a member of the armed forces, you can be called upon to go to war. You may have to kill people. Although the Canadian military generally focuses on peacekeeping and relief missions, there's always the possibility that you'll be called into combat.

The main comment I've heard regarding military training is this: If you want to be an Air Force pilot, join the Air Force. But if you want to be an airline pilot, do your training through a college or flight school, and work your way up into civil aviation. Although airlines tend to look favourably on pilot candidates with military experience, joining the military for the sole purpose of gaining experience is probably unwise. Not only will you have a long commitment before you are allowed to leave the Forces, it's possible that all your time will be spent flying helicopters—something that will not prepare you for a career with the airlines. That, combined with a lack of control over where you live, is unlikely to keep you happy. However, if you spend every night dreaming about flying a fighter jet, the military may be a good place for you. In fact, it may be the only place to do your training!

A Canadian Forces CF-18 Hornet
photo by James Ball

CHAPTER FOUR: STARTING YOUR TRAINING

As soon as we left the ground I knew I myself had to fly!

—Amelia Earhart

YOU'VE decided where you'll be doing your training, now comes the business of actually getting your licences. There are a number of steps that must be followed in order to receive your private pilot licence. The first, as discussed earlier, is to get a medical certificate. You should do this before any flight training so that you can deal with any unforeseen medical problems early on. Next, if you have chosen to do your training at a flight school, you'll have to choose an instructor. That instructor will be responsible for helping you pass the rest of the steps to get your licence. These include: obtaining a Radiotelephone Operator's Restricted Certificate (Aeronautical), passing your PSTAR written test, flying your first solo, writing the private pilot written exam, and passing the private pilot flight test.

Choosing Your Instructor

If you decide to attend a college aviation program, or if you're able to obtain your private licence through air cadets, you may not have much say as to who your instructor will be. However, if you decide to carry out your training through a traditional flight school, you have a choice as to who will be your instructor. Depending on the size of the flight school, you may be able choose from a large number of instructors. For the most part, you'll have one primary instructor for all your flight training. It's possible that your primary instructor will occasionally have another instructor fill in for them (like a substitute teacher), but that will usually only happen under extenuating circumstances. Having a single, regular instructor throughout the duration of your training can be highly beneficial— your training will have a familiarity, and your instructor will be aware of your strengths and weaknesses, and thus be able to tailor your training appropriately. It's important to find an instructor with whom you're comfortable.

Some people will argue that, since you'll be flying with numerous personality types throughout your career, you should try to get along with your flight instructor no matter what their personality and teaching style is like. I disagree. It's true that you may not get along with some of the pilots you may fly with in the future, but that's a completely different type of working relationship than the one you'll have with your instructor. After all, the purpose of a flight is to safely get from point A to point B (in commercial flying, anyway). In flight training, however, the purpose of the flight is to learn. In a commercial flight, the other pilot is just another employee, but in a training flight, the instructor is essentially working for you. You're paying them to teach you, and if they're not teaching you effectively, you're wasting your money.

Choosing an instructor can be a difficult and personal process, and you must be honest with yourself throughout. There are many important questions that need to be addressed. Do you want an instructor who is laid back, or do you want someone who will fire you up and get your butt in gear? Does it matter if they're male or female? What's their schedule and availability? Do not be afraid to interview a number of different instructors at the school to figure out who is best suited for the task. If you find your instructor's teaching style is unsuitable once your training has begun, do not be afraid to switch to another instructor. Jumping from instructor to instructor is not a good idea, but if you really dislike your instructor, it can be a wise decision when made early on.

For my private licence, I did not have a choice of instructors. Although my instructor was good, I felt his teaching style was not compatible with my learning style. I earned my private licence in the necessary time as required by my college, but I really did not enjoy my training as much as I should have. A good instructor can make the difference between simply working on your licence and having an amazing experience.

Hangar Talk – Choosing an Instructor

Don't be afraid to go to different instructors. It's your right as a customer, and one of the few times early in your aviation career when you will be treated with respect—because money talks.

—*Matt Hogan, Airbus A320 First Officer*

If you aren't happy with your current instructor, try a new one. You're the customer. If possible, train with an experienced instructor—preferably a Class 3, 2, or 1. Ask lots of questions. Talk to other students.

—*Mike McDonald, B1900 Captain, Skylink Express*

Radiotelephone Operator's Restricted Certificate (Aeronautical)

A Radiotelephone Operator's Restricted Certificate must be earned in order for you to use the two-way radio that comes standard in most planes. An airplane with a two-way radio has both a radio receiver and a radio transmitter. In order to transmit over a radio frequency, you must have a radiotelephone operator's certificate. This exam covers various topics such as proper radio procedures, technical operations, and the phonetic alphabet. Although the material is important to learn, the exam is really quite boring and is more of an inconvenience than anything else.

Your school will likely have a copy of the study guide. If it doesn't, the guide can be accessed through Industry Canada's website at:

http://strategis.ic.gc.ca/epic/internet/insmt-gst.nsf/en/sf01397e.html.

There's a general guide and a study guide specifically for the aeronautical certificate. Most of the questions will come from the aeronautical guide, but a few are sure to come from the general guide. Therefore, it's a good idea to familiarize yourself with both.

Practice using the phonetic alphabet whenever you can. You'll seem like an extreme pilot geek while doing so, but the quicker you can commit the alphabet to memory the better. I found it was helpful to look at licence plates while driving and say what the plates were in the phonetic alphabet. Alternatively, if you're on the phone and you need to spell something, use this alphabet. On a side note unrelated to the radio operator's exam, if you are able to learn Morse code, you will impress your instructor. Nowadays it is not used very often, but it still would not hurt to know it.

PSTAR

The first few flying lessons you have will be dual lessons with your instructor. He or she will go through all the basics of flight and operations for your particular airport. It's not necessary for me to go over all the different lessons they will be teaching you. The main advice I'll offer is that after each lesson, make sure you go over it in your head and do as much studying as possible before your next lesson. Flight time is expensive and you have a lot of information thrown at you in your first few lessons. Studying at home allows you to better absorb the information and be better prepared for future lessons. Also, don't be surprised if a handful of your early lessons are spent in the circuit where you simply take-off, fly back parallel to the runway, and land. Although sometimes monotonous, these early lessons are vital preparation for your first solo flight. Before flying solo you must obtain your student pilot permit by writing and passing the PSTAR. PSTAR doesn't stand for anything but rather is the computer code given to the Student Pilot Permit Aviation Regulation Examination.

The PSTAR test consists of fifty multiple-choice questions, ninety percent of which must be answered correctly in order to pass.

This may seem daunting, but the fifty questions are selected word-for-word from 200 sample questions that can be found in the Student Pilot Permit study guide, which is available online:

http://www.tc.gc.ca/civilaviation/general/Exams/guides/tp11919/General.htm

The guide covers a number of different areas, including:

+ Canadian Aviation Regulations (CARs)
+ Air Traffic Control Clearances and Instructions
+ Air Traffic Control procedures as they apply to the control of VFR traffic
+ Air Traffic procedures at uncontrolled airports and aerodromes
+ Special VFR Regulations
+ Aeronautical Information Circulars
+ NOTAM

The tricky part of The Transport Canada guide is that it doesn't provide the answers to each of the questions. Instead, it points you to the CARs and the Airman's Information Manual (AIM), where the answers can be found. Although I recommend you search through the databases to familiarize yourself with both, they can be quite confusing and the answers are sometimes difficult to find. There are, however, a number of online study guides. One of the most effective, and the one that I would recommend, can be found here:

http://fly.wabyn.net/FlightTraining/PSTAR/PSTARIndex.htm.

Study guides are great for confirming what the correct answer is, but they're not a substitute for going and finding the answer on your own. This test forms the foundation of aviation regulation knowledge and the information tested is important. If you have any questions regarding the test, be sure to ask your instructor. If you happen to fail the PSTAR, you can write it again using a different version of the test.

The First Solo

After passing your PSTAR, Radiotelephone operator's cert-ificate, and a school and aircraft ground-school test, your instructor will start preparing you for your solo. The first solo usually comes after you've flown roughly ten to fifteen hours. Don't worry if it takes you a little longer, as there are numerous factors involved in determining when you are ready. It doesn't mean you're a bad pilot. Conversely, if you happen to solo earlier than most, don't go thinking you're the next Top Gun! There will be a number of re-quired exercises that you must practice before your instructor will let you solo. Besides general aircraft handling skills, you'll be required to know your emergency procedures, how to recover from a stall, how to perform a cross-wind landing, how to fly an overshoot or rejected landing, and how to deal with a runway change mid-circuit. Take the time to do some hangar flying, by sitting in the plane with everything turned off and practicing emergency procedures and each phase of flight. It really helps.

Every pilot remembers his or her first solo. The sheer exhil-aration of being completely in control of a flying aircraft is an amazing feeling. Depending on your instructor, you may have an idea what day you'll be going up, or they may surprise you. I've known a number of people who, after flying a couple of dual circuits, had their instructor say to them, "Ok, how about you drop me off and go for a circuit by yourself." If you have a newly qualified instructor, he or she may get a more experienced instructor to fly with you for a circuit or two before you can solo. It's not an indication of your flying skill. Instructors will not allow you to solo if they don't feel you're ready. They will also not allow you to solo if you yourself do not feel ready. Some instructors will tell you that they're often more nervous than their students during that first solo flight. You may see instructors in the airport lounge, looking worriedly out the window as a student flies by on their first solo.

Continuing Lessons

Now that you've gotten the solo out of the way, you can concentrate on getting your private licence. The flight test for the private licence is quite extensive. Many items on the test have specific pass/fail limits, and are tested individually. For example, in a steep turn, you must maintain your altitude within +/- 100 ft and your airspeed within +/- ten knots. During both your solo and dual lessons, you'll be practicing these manoeuvres and items. When you're flying solo, it can be tempting to try and just fly-around and sightsee. I know that I had a few solo flights where I didn't really feel like doing any stalls or steep turns, and instead just flew around taking advantage of the fact that I, alone, was in control of an airplane. While I recommend that people take time to appreciate the privilege of flying, doing this too much can really hinder your progress towards obtaining a licence.

On your solo flights, I recommend setting out a checklist for yourself. Set goals. Decide which flight-test items you want to practice and what standards you want to set for yourself. When it's almost time to take the test, raise your standards even higher than the testing standards. For the step turn example above, if the flight test standards are +/- 100 ft, set your standards at +/- 50 ft. After you've completed the checklist, take some time to explore your local area.

The Cross-Country

The phrase *cross-country flying* is often misunderstood. It does not mean flying from coast to coast, it means flying from one place to another or going to a different airport. Unlike training flights where you will likely stay close to your home airport, cross-country flights provide you an opportunity to go to other airports. I really liked this part of my training, as it not only offers a change of scenery, but is also the type of flying that is closest to "real airline" flying. When someone would ask what I did today, I always enjoyed responding, "Oh, I just flew to Ottawa and back."

Cross-Country flying has its challenges. Flight planning and fuel calculations can be tricky and very time consuming when first starting out. Drawing the routes onto your maps and picking checkpoints can also be time consuming. Give yourself plenty of time for pre-flight planning and practice it regularly. Try planning for theoretical cross-country flights even if you'll not be flying to that particular place. It's good practice, and you may get to fly that route when you're trying to build time for your commercial licence.

When doing your cross-country flights or regular exercises, be sure to practice diversions. Challenge yourself. This is something that may one day save your life. A diversion is when you change your destination mid-flight. This may be because of bad weather, a mechanical problem, or maybe you just really need to go to the bathroom! There are GPS receivers in modern flying, and they're invaluable in aiding diversion calculations, but it's still an essential skill to know how to perform diversions the old-fashioned way. According to Murphy's law, the one day you run into bad weather is the day that your GPS decides to quit, so you must always be prepared. The Chief Pilot at my old airline would often do ride-alongs with random pilots. Sometimes, in the middle of the flight, he would switch off the GPS and say, "Ok, get us to the destination and give me an estimate for when we'll get there." You'd better get him there, and close to your estimated ETA, or there will be repercussions.

The Private Pilot Written Exam

After you've completed ten hours of flight training, forty hours of ground school, and have a letter of recommendation from your flight instructor, you're eligible to take the private pilot licence written exam. Although I would not personally recommend taking this test so early in your training, it may not be a bad idea to get the written test out of the way.

The testing for the private pilot licence contains two parts: A flight test, which will be discussed later, and a multiple-choice exam administered by Transport Canada. If you haven't noticed already, you will have to complete (and pass) many written exams throughout your flying career. The exam consists of 100 questions, and you must score at least sixty percent to pass. The exam is broken up into four sections:

1. Air Law: Air Law & Procedures
2. Navigation: Navigation & Radio Aids
3. Meteorology: Meteorology
4. Aeronautics & General Knowledge:
    a. Airframes, Engines & Systems
    b. Theory of Flight
    c. Flight Instruments
    d. Flight Operations
    e. Human Factors

You must score sixty percent or higher on each section of the exam, so if you excel in three sections only to fail in another, you will not pass, regardless of your overall score.

Transport Canada has put out a study guide for all exams. The study guide for the private pilot examination can be accessed online:

http://www.tc.gc.ca/CivilAviation/general/exams/guides/tp12 880/menu.htm

I recommend looking at it. It may also be helpful to use commercial study guides to review, find practice questions, and study condensed information. Michael Culhane has a series of study guides for each of the different flight tests. While expensive, I highly recommend utilizing this resource. Usually there are two books, one with practice exams and the other with concentrated study guides. The books are well laid out, with each question in the practice exams referencing the location of the explanation in the study guide. Some people will find the books more helpful than others. I find I learn best if I can do numerous practice questions, and these books worked out great for that. You'll even find that a few of the questions from the study book are worded exactly as they are on the actual exam. Others are the same question with different values. These books can be found at:

http://www.acceleratedaviation.com/

Transport Canada has also published *The Art of Writing an Examination*. This publication includes valuable tips for writing an aviation exam.

The Art of Writing an Examination

These exam-writing tips have been compiled as a result of a group workshop held during Instructor Refresher Course #147 (Toronto, May 1998). This list will be useful to candidates preparing for and writing a Transport Canada flight crew examination.

Physical and Mental Preparation

+ Do not 'cram'- especially the morning of the exam.
+ Try to duplicate the exam environment when you study (in other words, do not study in bed).
+ Write a practice exam.
+ Do you need an appointment to write the exam.?
+ Organize tools the day before the exam.
+ Get plenty of sleep and eat properly.
+ Limit caffeine intake.

Getting There

+ Allow extra time / plan to arrive early.
+ Plan route/ drive slowly.
+ Dress comfortably.
+ Consider availability of parking.

What to Bring

+ I.D., current medical, letter of recommendation, proof of experience and training.
+ Appropriate payment.
+ Pencils, eraser, navigation ruler, protractor.
+ Approved calculator, flight computer.

At the Counter

- ✈ Confirm you have brought all the required items (see above).
- ✈ Smile/be polite.
- ✈ Ask questions/confirm any ambiguities.
- ✈ Confirm you're writing the correct exam (English, French, Both).
- ✈ Confirm you have the correct appendices, maps, abbreviation list, and dictionary.
- ✈ Be prepared for delays at the desk.
- ✈ Have a good attitude.

Getting Organized in the Room

- ✈ Expect one-way mirrors or surveillance cameras.
- ✈ Organize your tools/take a few deep breaths.
- ✈ Write down formulae that you think you might forget.
- ✈ Take time to read the instructions carefully.
- ✈ Scan the entire exam before answering any questions.

Time Management

- ✈ Note your starting time and keep track of your time as you go along.
- ✈ Do not rush.
- ✈ Save time-consuming, difficult questions until the end.
- ✈ Do not dwell on questions you are unsure of/keep going.
- ✈ Save time for review at the end.
- ✈ It's not necessary to fill out a flight log.

Getting Help

- ✈ If you need help, ask right away (for example, when a question is smudged, your pen runs dry, your computer or calculator breaks, or you need more paper, etc.).

Reading the Question

- Read every word.
- Read the question at least twice before answering.
- Understand what's being asked/check for key words.
- Cover the answers until you formulate your answer.
- Draw a picture if it will help you visualize the situation.
- If computations are involved, estimate the answer, and then compute it exactly.

The Four Responses/Answering the Question

- Consider each answer as a true or false statement.
- Use a process of elimination.
- Choose the most correct response.
- Double-check the number on the answer sheet.

"How Goes It" List

- Do the easy questions first.
- Make a list of unsure and unanswered questions.
- Keep your eyes on the time.

Final Check

- Answer all questions/do not leave any questions blank.

Source: *The Art of Writing an Examination*
URL: **http://www.tc.gc.ca/CivilAviation/General/Exams/Art.htm,**
Civil Aviation, May 1998. Reproduced with the permission of the Minister of Public Works and Government Services Canada, 2007.

The final piece of advice I'll offer for this exam is **BE PRE-PARED**. There really is no excuse for insufficient preparation prior to your private test. If you're at a flight college and the test is scheduled in advance, you know roughly when it will be, and you should be studying well in advance. If your training is at a flight school, you may have the opportunity to write the exam on your own time. Do not write the exam if you do not feel ready. Personally, I would try to write a last practice exam from a study book a week before the test. This will give you a good idea where you are in your preparation, and will allow you enough time to spend the last few days studying your weaker subjects.

The Private Pilot Flight Test

Your first flight test can be quite intimidating. In fact, there are seasoned airline pilots who still dread their check rides, even though they've probably completed well over twenty-five during their careers. A flight test is like a driving test on steroids. There are numerous items to cover and you never know exactly what things will be covered until the actual day of the test. Combine that with the uncertainty of the weather, and you have a situation where you can end up driving yourself nuts with anticipation. Nevertheless, flight tests do not have to be that nerve-wracking. Most of the Designated Flight Test Examiners (DFTE) that you'll fly with are very nice people who understand the stress you're under, and are not out to fail you. Your instructor has to officially recommend you to take your flight test. He or she would not do so if they didn't feel you were capable of passing the test. As long as you've been practicing and have studied your material, you'll do fine.

In order to be eligible for a private pilot flight test, you need a recommendation from your flight instructor. You'll also need to have completed over 35 hours of flight time, including the specific requirements outlined below. However, the licence will not be issued until you have passed the written and flight tests and completed over 45 hours of flight time. It is generally quite unusual for someone to obtain their licence with that low an hour total so do not be discouraged if it takes you a little longer. The actual flying portion of a flight test usually lasts anywhere between sixty to ninety minutes in the air. Flight tests will also include some pre-flight discussion questions on rules of the air and navigation. You'll have to plan a flight as if you were flying cross-country, and the DFTE will likely ask you questions about the route you chose and your way points. If they question you on something, it does not mean that you're wrong; they are likely just trying to determine your reasoning.

If you fail two or more exercises during your flight test, yet your overall score is still high enough to achieve a pass, you'll receive what's known as a "partial." This means that you neither officially passed nor failed the test. You have an opportunity within thirty days to go up with an examiner and repeat those exercises (and only those exercises) that you failed in your initial test.

Occasionally, a DFTE will want to use the flight test as an opportunity to teach you something new. If this happens, and your DFTE introduces you to something unfamiliar, there's no need to worry. During my private flight test, the examiner unexpectedly asked, "So, you're flying in Mexico and your medical expires—what do you do?" I was honest with him and said I had no clue, and then reminded him that I make a point of checking my medical expiry before going on any long-distance flights. Even still, I learned something new, and thanks to my examiner's line of questioning, I learned exactly what to do in the hypothetical scenario posed: I should call the Canadian Embassy and they would supply me with a list of approved medical examiners in my immediate area.

After the ground portion, you will head out to the aircraft. Depending on the situation, you may have done a walk-around before the ground portion on your own or with the examiner watching. Don't be surprised if they ask you questions about the aircraft during the walk-around. Make sure you know all the parts: where the antennas are, what the antennas do, where the drains are, and what colour each light is. Your instructor should give you a practice walk-around before the actual test. Once you've finished your walk-around, take your time getting everything ready. Do all your pre-flight checks. *Do not hurry.*

There are a number of books on what to do (and not do) during the in-flight portion of your flight test. Your instructor should go over each part with you as well so you know what to expect. During your test, it's important to take your time. Do not feel rushed. If you think you screwed up on any given section, don't dwell on it. If you truly screwed up on a section, the worst-case scenario is that you'll receive a partial fail and will be required to take the failed section again. Don't be devastated if, overall, you fail the test. There are plenty of airline pilots who failed their first private pilot flight-test— it's not the end of your flying career. It will never come up in future job interviews. Except for being out a little extra cash, it shouldn't cause you undue stress. Be sure to try to get a good night's sleep the night before the exam and try to keep nerves in check. Spend the time before your test doing some mild hangar flying, going over each procedure in your head. As long as you focus on each procedure that you are working on, you'll do fine.

The Transport Canada flight test guide for the private pilot flight test is found online at:

http://www.tc.gc.ca/civilaviation/general/flttrain/Planes/Pubs/TP 13723/menu.htm

Experience Requirements

As per the Canadian Aviation Regulations, the experience requirements for the awarding of a private pilot licence are:

(a) An applicant shall have completed a minimum of 45 hours private pilot flight training in airplanes under the direction and supervision of a Flight Instructor. A maximum 5 of the 45 hours may be conducted on an approved airplane simulator or flight training device.

(b) The flight training shall include a minimum of:

(i) 17 hours dual instruction flight time, including a minimum of 3 hours cross-country flight time and 5 hours of instrument time, of which a maximum of 3 hours may be in a simulator or flight-training device; and
(ii) 12 hours solo flight time, including 5 hours cross-country flight time with a flight of a minimum of 150 nautical miles, which shall include 2 full stop landings at points other than the point of departure.

Standards

Although you only need to meet the private pilot standards to pass your flight test, I would highly recommend that you attempt to keep your flying performance within commercial standards while doing your training. For example, the requirement for basic instrument flying underneath "the hood" (a device which limits your outside view), in the private pilot flight test is that you stay within +/- 200 ft of the assigned altitude. For the commercial flight test, you need to maintain +/- 100 ft of the assigned altitude. In your practicing, don't be content with your ability to maintain +/- 200 ft. Aim to keep it within 100 ft at the most, based on the commercial standard (although ultimately, you should be aiming to remain exactly on the directed altitude at all times). In fact, in military flight training, if you are told to keep an assigned altitude, they want the plane *exactly* at that altitude, not +/- 100 ft or even 50 ft! In your training, challenge yourself and set your standards high.

CHAPTER FIVE: BECOMING A COMMERCIAL PILOT

You can always tell when a man has lost his soul to flying. The poor bastard is hopelessly committed to stopping whatever he is doing long enough to look up and make sure the aircraft purring overhead continues on course and does not suddenly fall out of the sky. It is also his bound duty to watch every aircraft within view take off and land.

—Ernest K Gann, 'Fate is the Hunter.'

AFTER you've obtained your private licence, you need to decide if you're going to work towards your commercial licence and become a career pilot. If you're in a college aviation program, this decision will be far easier because college aviation programs cater to this very situation. You will simply continue in your current program. Nevertheless, if you haven't done so already, now is the time to start your professional training by acting professionally. You should start treating your commercial training as if it were a job.

As you will see, many of your jobs in aviation will be based on word of mouth and networking. Instructors, fellow students, airport employees, and even flight-test examiners will observe the attitude you display during your training. For this reason, it's imperative that you strive to impress. Be sure to show up on time for all your lessons—if you must cancel, provide adequate notice. As a flight instructor, there's nothing worse than having a lesson booked, making your way to the airport, and then discovering your student is a no-show. Your instructor is almost certainly someone who's trying to progress in the industry, just like you. In fact, sometimes they will be only a few years ahead of you. Your instructor is likely to become one of your best contacts in the industry, and somewhere down the road, they may be in a position to recommend you for a job or inform you of a recently vacated position. If their memories of you are unpleasant and include a number of no-shows, they may be less inclined to give you the leg-up that could later prove to be invaluable.

Showing up for lessons on time is essential, but you must also show up prepared. One of the most important concepts in flying is to "remain ahead of the aircraft." Knowing ahead of time what you need to do, at what altitude you need to be, and what radio frequency you need to dial, are all vital to the safety and success of the flight. This concept extends to pre-flight as well. Do your reading, flight planning, and studying well ahead of time. Be comfortable with the concepts you ought to know cold, and if you have questions, write them down and ask your instructor when there is an opportunity to do so. This will make lessons run more smoothly, increase your enjoyment, and impress your instructor. Studying and practicing pre-flight planning and research is a necessary part of learning. It can be frustrating for an instructor to see potential in a student, and to see that potential wasted due to the lack of hard work. One of their goals is to help you attain your commercial licence; if you never reach your goal because you lack discipline, it shows a great disrespect to your instructor.

It's also important to present yourself professionally to other people at the airport. You never know who might be watching. You'll never be completely anonymous, despite what you may think. How strangers perceive you could have a bearing on your future success in finding jobs. Do you come to your training appropriately dressed, groomed, and looking professional? Do you treat the front desk staff, the line crew, and maintenance workers politely and respectfully? Are you responsible with your decisions about when to fly and when not to? Although only a student, you're training to be a professional, and while certain sections of the industry have different ideas of what the make-up of a professional is, it's imperative that you work towards being one.

Networking

If you've not yet begun the process of building up your contacts list, doing so now, while you train, would be prudent. Networking is important in most professions and the same holds true in aviation. Very often, jobs emerge via word-of-mouth or personal recommendations. Translation: increasing your connections increases your chances of securing a job in the future. How difficult the networking process proves to be depends largely on your personality. On the surface, networking is nothing more than meeting new people. However, subtle communication skills also come into play.

While I do not claim to be an expert when it comes to networking, I've managed to develop some guidelines over the years. Guidelines that I believe can work for everyone. Most of my jobs have been procured through some form of networking, and so it would be sheer negligence on my part to underestimate the importance of this topic.

Proper networking is not necessarily planned ahead of time in every case. You probably won't wake up one morning and say, "I'm going to meet someone today who'll benefit my career in a couple years." For example, you shouldn't go up to a chief pilot and say, "I am looking for a job, can I buy you a drink and have you hire me?" Instead, networking is a way of thinking, a way of keeping yourself open to the opportunities around you. It's your willingness to explore new people and new situations that will allow you to master networking.

The easiest type of networking is direct interaction. This happens most often with your fellow students, your professors, and your instructors. Spending so much time with these people will inevitably lead to close, working relationships. It's here that students attending a college aviation program may have an advantage over those attending a traditional flight school, as they'll often spend two or three years with the same students and instructors, and therefore be able to develop closer friendships. At a traditional flight school, on the other hand, there may be the potential to meet a greater number of people—this is dependent on the size of your school and of the size of the airport where you're based. However, in a traditional flight school environment, you're likely to see less of your fellow students, which can make networking more difficult.

Some of your best contacts will be with aviation staff who are located in other cities, or who are based out of other airports. They're the toughest contacts to make, since they move in different social and professional circles, but this is also their strength. By networking with people all over the country, you'll no longer be limiting yourself to work being offered in your immediate area. Your long-distance contacts will be able to inform you of new opportunities in their respective areas. Better still, they may recommend you to their superiors. To give yourself the best opportunity of making long-distance contacts, socialize with staff at airports other than your own, whenever the opportunity arises. Not every conversation you start will turn into a contact, but I think you'll be surprised how many of them do.

So, while you cannot always be in a position to meet a potential contact, you can plan to be in a position where you increase your chances. While working on your commercial licence, don't just come into the airport, complete your flight, and go home. Try to come in early or stay late, have a snack at the airport cafeteria, or spend some time just hanging out plane watching. It would also be advantageous for you to find a job at the airport. Working as a line crew agent not only immerses you in the industry and gives you experience for a potential ramp job, but it also gives you a chance to meet different pilots, students, and aircraft owners. Numerous jobs in and around the airport provide a great opportunity to meet people.

Successful networking is not a guarantee to finding your dream job, but when combined with a solid reputation, it will dramatically increase your chances. So many jobs are passed along by word-of-mouth, and so many jobs in aviation are dependent on recommendations from someone already in the company. There are two key aspects involved in these types of recommendations. Not only is it important for a contact to know you, they also must have good things to say about you.

Hangar Talk – Networking

Aviation is all about networking and appearances. You need to get out into the industry and meet people.
> —*Darlene Sly, Twin Otter First Officer – Winward Island Airways*

Networking is good. Don't burn bridges, and be nice.
> —*Altaf Rashid, B1900 Captain – Falcon Express Cargo Airlines*

During college I worked at the dispatch desk at the local flight school where I got my "Rec" permit. I developed a good relationship with the Chief Flight Instructor and started my first instructing job as soon as I was done with college.
> —*Julie Beverstein, B1900D First Officer – Georgian Airways*

Make as many contacts as you can throughout your training, and follow up on all of them. Try like hell to speak with or meet the chief pilot and present yourself as a motivated, educated, intelligent person. FOLLOW UP routinely with the contacts you have made. Just dropping off a resume and moving on does not show sufficient motivation. Stay positive...with the right attitude anyone can make it in this industry.
> —*Geoff Cattrall, A340/A330 Second Officer – Cathay Pacific*

Working at the Airport

While you work towards your commercial licence, it's not a bad idea to try and get a job at the airport. I didn't do this during my training. I was still able to become a commercial pilot, but I think it would have been easier applying for jobs if I could have included this experience on my résumé. There are many things to consider should you decide to seek employment to accompany your training. Besides the obvious financial question—would an airport job pay enough?—it's also important to take networking potential into consideration. What opportunity for contacts will the airport job offer you? Will the job give you experience that future employers are likely to find attractive?

Having a job that allows you to meet other pilots, specifically at a general aviation level, will put you in a good position to hear industry gossip. Jobs at local airport flying clubs or Fixed Base Operators (FBOs),which are essentially gas stations and private terminals for general aviation aircraft, are probably the best way to get your foot in the door and to meet the most people. Many of these jobs will also allow you to become familiar with the airport environment, which will be useful in your first flying job. Don't be annoying or pushy, but be sure to tactfully mention to people that you're working on your pilot's licence and will be looking for a flying job at some point. You never know who *they* may know.

Non-flying jobs with major airlines are less beneficial. Yes, it may help you further down the road when you're an established pilot looking for work, but when you're just starting out and hunting for that first job, it will be of no real value. While the airline benefits are nice, this type of job will not build your contact base as much as if you were working in a general aviation environment. However, working for a major airline is still a great way to learn the industry.

Informing Thy Self

Attempting to meet new people and network can be tough if you have nothing to say. While working on your commercial licence, you should try to find out as much as you can about how the industry works—news, key issues, how business is going for specific airlines, and anything else that may be of interest to pilots. There are a number of resources for this, the most common being magazines and websites.

Magazines include:
Wings Magazine: http://www.wingsmagazine.com/
Canadian Aviator: http://www.canadianaviatormagazine.com/
Flying Magazine: http://www.flyingmag.com/
Aviation Week & Space Technology: www.aviationnow.com

Websites include:
http://www.avcanada.ca/ – The Online Forums are a great way to learn industry gossip, but be sure to take everything that is said with

a grain of salt—often the anonymous format of the forum provides ways for people to blow off some steam.

http://www.jetthrust.com/ – A similar online forum, slightly tamer.

http://www.pprune.org/ – A British-based aviation forum.

http://www.avweb.com/ – A US based Aviation news service.

http://www.pilotcareercentre.com/ – also a great resource, not only for learning which airlines are hiring, but also for discovering where airlines are located and what type of aircraft they operate.

In-flight Training

Acting professionally, networking, and immersing yourself in the industry are all important aspects of getting your licence, but flight training is still the most important. Similar to the private licence, you are required to pass a flight test and a written exam after achieving a minimum of 200 hours. Building hours towards your commercial licence is an expensive proposition, so make these hours useful. Although you want to ensure you have the basics for your flight test down, practicing steep turns when you already know how to do them isn't a good use of your hours, and isn't a good use of the money spent to pay for those hours. There are a number of ways in which you can build your hours productively, which will not simply meet the minimum hours required, but will provide other benefits as well. With some college programs, you may be limited in what you can do during your flights, but there are still ways to make your flights productive.

Building hours is expensive. Now that you have your private licence, try to offset the costs of flying by taking friends with you on the flights. If you plan a cross-country flight for a day trip, you can often get your passenger to split the costs with you. This way, you not only get to spend a fun day with friends and give them an interesting experience, but you can also subsidize your hours. You'll be amazed by the high number of people interested in going for flights in a small plane. One small caveat: you do not yet have your commercial licence, and so you cannot generate actual revenue on the flight—your friends are only allowed to reimburse the cost of the flight.

Besides making your flights more affordable, you'll also want to find ways to make your flights more productive, thus making you more employable in the future. At this point in your training, you should be both networking *and* thinking about the different types of flying that you want to do in the future, and tailoring your training accordingly. For example, if you think that you'd like to start off by flying floats, try to find somewhere that rents float planes after you get your initial rating. If you're able to build up your total hours and your float hours at the same time, you'll have a better chance of finding a float-flying job when you're done. Some float operators have fifty-hour float rating courses that may be a viable option. The initial float rating only requires seven hours on floats, but you'll be very hard-pressed to find operators that will hire a float plane pilot with only seven hours' experience. As a result, some schools offer a way to achieve fifty hours on floats in addition to offering some practical real-world training. These courses are significantly more expensive than gaining the hours on a conventional-wheel aircraft, but it may make you much more employable when you're done. If this is a route you think you'd like to take, be proactive. In the next chapter, I'll discuss the concept of researching companies. In the case of the above example, though, try to find float operators who you think would make good employers, and ask them if they recommend taking a float course and if there are any particular courses that they recommend.

You should also be using your cross-country flights to visit potential employers. This can be tricky and requires A LOT of advanced planning, but if you can drop off résumés and meet Chief Pilots before you've obtained your licence, you'll have a better idea of what opportunities await you following the completion of your training. You'll also have a better chance of being remembered by the Chief Pilot when you send your résumé and are actively seeking employment.

It's a relatively minor point, but I have heard numerous pilots say that they wish that they had done this in their training. One of the requirements to get an Airline Transport Licence is to have 25 hours of night P.I.C. (pilot in command) Cross Country time. Even though this hour total is relatively low, it can be quite difficult to obtain. When you start off flying as a job, you'll likely be flying as a co-pilot (and therefore not logging P.I.C. time) or if you are flying as a Captain, you'll likely be flying a single engine wheel or float plane. On floats, you're not allowed to land or take-off at night and on wheels, for most single engine planes you're not allowed to carry revenue passengers at night. Therefore, it's entirely possible that you will have flown for a number of years and have a couple thousand hours with less than 25 night cross country P.I.C. hours. While working on your commercial, after you've received your night rating, try and do as many cross countries flights as possible at night. This way, you can not only be building hours towards your commercial licence, but you can possibly make it much easier for yourself when you go to get your ATPL later on in your career. Some schools have curfews, and therefore the opportunity for night flying is limited. There are ways around this, though. It's possible, for example, to plan your flights for later in the day. By doing this, the sun will set while you're still airborne, which allows you to count those hours as night flying hours.

There is one final aspect of commercial flight training to keep in mind: make sure to have fun! After you start flying for profit, it's rare that you would get to choose where or when you're going to fly. Take advantage of this opportunity now and relish it. One of the dreams of aviation is to have the luxury of taking your own private plane, and going where you want, when you want. So, while you have to opportunity, and have to spend the money to get your commercial licence anyways, use that luxury.

Different Ratings

As mentioned in the first chapter, there are different ratings that you can add to a private licence. While you're building up hours for your commercial licence, it's a good idea to start working towards these other ratings. Night rating, float rating, multi-engine rating, and an IFR rating can all be added to your private licence.

Night Rating:

More than half of all commercial flights in the world have at least some flight-time during darkness. Therefore, to be a commercial pilot, a night rating is required. There are a number of differences between flying at night and flying during the day, and Transport Canada requires a separate rating to fly after dark.

The requirements are:

An applicant for a night rating shall have acquired, in aeroplanes, a minimum of 20 hours of pilot flight time, which shall include a minimum of:
(i) 10 hours of night flight time including a minimum of:
   (A) 5 hours dual flight time, including 2 hours of cross-country flight time,
   (B) 5 hours solo flight time, including 10 takeoffs, circuits, landings, and
(ii) 10 hours dual instrument time.
(iii) Credit for a maximum of 5 of the 10 hours of dual instrument time may be given for instrument ground time, provided that the total instrument time is not in addition to the 10 hours night flight time in subparagraph (a)(i) above.

Multi-Engine Rating:

There is not a set number of hours required in order to obtain a multi-engine rating. There are, however, other specific requirements that need to be met in the training. Your training for the multi-engine rating does not have to be with a flight instructor. In fact, you can complete the training with any pilot who holds both a valid multi-engine rating, and a valid commercial licence with fifty-plus hours of multi-engine time. Despite this leniency in the training laws, I'd recommend that you complete all the necessary training with only qualified instructors. Approximately five to fifteen hours of training is generally required to cover everything that will be featured in the multi-engine flight test. One requirement of training for a multi-engine rating is that the student has to experience an actual intentional engine shut down in flight. The first time you're in a multi-engine plane and you turn one of the engines off, it is quite a sight as generally the *last* thing you want to see when 5000 ft in the air is one of your propellers stop turning!

Seaplane Rating:

In order to fly a float plane—a plane that can land or take off on the water—a pilot is required to have a seaplane rating.

(i) An applicant for a seaplane rating shall complete a total of 7 hours of seaplane training, including:
    (A) a minimum of 5 hours dual instruction
    (B) a minimum of 5 takeoffs and landings as sole occupant of the aeroplane, except for two crew aircraft, in which case the takeoffs and landings shall be done as pilot-in-command.
(ii) The following exercises shall be included in the seaplane training:
    (A) taxiing,
    (B) sailing,
    (C) docking,
    (D) takeoffs,
    (E) landings, and
    (F) as conditions exist, operations on glassy water, rough water, and in cross-wind conditions.

Instrument Rating:

The initial private pilot licence allows pilots to fly VFR (visual flight rules). When you are flying VFR, you fly with visual reference to the ground. In order to fly in clouds, or IFR (Instrument Flight Rules), pilots are required to obtain an Instrument Rating.

a) Knowledge
An applicant shall have obtained a minimum of 70% on the written examination Instrument Rating (INRAT), which shall include the following subjects:
    (i) *Canadian Aviation Regulations*;
    (ii) Instrument Flight Rules and Procedures;
    (iii) Meteorology;
    (iv) Instruments;
    (v) Radio and Radar systems; and
    (vi) Navigation.

(b) **Experience**

An applicant shall have completed a minimum of:

(i) 50 hours of cross-country flight as pilot-in-command in aeroplanes or helicopters, of which 10 hours must be in the appropriate category; and

(ii) 40 hours of instrument time, of which a maximum of 20 hours may be instrument ground time. The 40 hours instrument time shall include a minimum of:

(A) 5 hours of dual instrument flight time, acquired from the holder of a flight instructor rating,

(B) 5 hours in aeroplanes where the applicant is applying for a Group 1, 2, or 3 instrument rating, or in helicopters where the applicant is applying for a Group 4 instrument rating,

(C) 15 hours of dual instrument flight time provided by a qualified person,

(D) one dual cross-country flight under simulated or actual IMC conditions of a minimum of one hundred nautical miles—the flight to be conducted in accordance with an IFR flight plan to include at two different locations, an instrument approach to minima.

(c) **Skill**

An applicant shall successfully complete:

(i) a flight test in accordance with the *Flight Test Standards— Instrument Rating* or,

(ii) a Pilot Proficiency Check (PPC) for operations under IFR (will be discussed in Chapter 7).

(iii) an applicant who successfully completes a Line Operational Evaluation (LOE) from an approved Advanced Qualification Program (AQP) is considered to have met the Part VI or Part VII pilot proficiency check. (airline operations)

The Commercial Pilot Licence Written Exam

After you complete forty hours of ground school, complete one-hundred hours of flight time (half of the hours required for your licence), and have a letter of recommendation from your instructor, you will be eligible to write the commercial pilot written exam. The commercial written exam is similar to the private pilot written exam, but is slightly longer and more in-depth. The exam consists of one-hundred questions, and you must get sixty percent correct to pass. The exam is broken up into four sections:

Air Law   - Air Law & Procedures
Navigation   - Navigation & Radio Aids
Meteorology   - Meteorology
Aeronautics & General Knowledge
                           -Airframes, Engines & Systems
                           -Theory of Flight
                           -Flight Instruments
                           -Flight Operations
                           -Human Factors

Similar to the Private Pilot Written Exam, you are required to score at least sixty percent on each individual section, so even if your overall score is well above sixty percent, you will not pass if you fail even one of the sections.

Refer to the previous chapter for general tips on how to succeed on a Transport Canada written exam. If you're writing the exam through a college, you'll know the date when you'll be writing the exam. Set up a study schedule so that you have lots of time to prepare. The last thing you need is to panic the night before a written exam. If you're responsible for setting the date yourself, try to give yourself a timeframe as to when you want to write it and adjust your studying schedule accordingly. Do not take the exam until you are well-prepared and feel you're ready.

The Commercial Pilot Licence Flight Test

The Commercial Pilot Licence Flight Test is like a deluxe version of the Private Pilot Licence Flight Test. The in-flight manoeuvres required are similar, but with higher standards. You'll almost certainly be asked a higher number of emergency and informational questions. The examiner wants to know that you're qualified to fly passengers for hire.

Transport Canada has a comprehensive online guide to the flight test requirements and exercises. It's available at:

http://www.tc.gc.ca/civilaviation/general/flttrain/Planes/Pubs/TP 13462/menu.htm

Be sure to review the guide in-depth before taking your flight test. If you've practiced your air work diligently and passed your private pilot flight test with no problems, you should pass your commercial exam with ease. As with the private flight test, the "partial pass" policy is also applicable to the commercial exam.

Experience Requirements

In order to receive a commercial licence, a pilot must have completed 200 flight hours in an airplane, with at least one-hundred hours of PIC time. Twenty hours of cross-country PIC time is also required. In addition, a commercial pilot licence candidate must have received the following:

-35 hours of dual instruction by a flight instructor that includes:
    -5 hours of dual night flying, including 2 hours of night cross country time
    -5 hours of dual cross country flight time
    -20 hours of instrument time, of which a maximum of ten hours can be conducted on a simulator.

-30 hours solo time that includes:
    -25 hours for the general improvement of flying skills

-a cross country flight to a destination over 300 NM away
that includes a total of three stops (DON'T forget to bring
your log book with you so you can get it stamped!).
-5 hours solo flight time by night, during which a minimum
of 10 takeoffs, circuits, and landings were completed.

The Webster Trophy

While working towards your commercial licence, you may want
to consider entering the Webster Memorial Trophy Competition.
The Webster Trophy is given out annually to the best amateur pilot
in Canada, decided by a series of ground, planning and in-flight tests.
The trophy was named after John C. Webster, a pilot who repre-
sented Canada in international aerobatic flying competitions. He lost
his life in an accident in 1931. His father created the competition the
following year in John's memory. Although it has faced disruption
because of the war and spiralling administrative costs, the Canadian
Sport Aeroplane Association revived the competition in 1980, with
modifications. The winner of the competition not only receives a
headset and round trip tickets to any Air Canada destination, but also
has the distinction of being named the best amateur pilot in Canada
—not a bad thing to have on your résumé! Many past winners are
now flying for Air Canada.

To enter the competition, you must be a Canadian citizen, a
British subject, or a landed immigrant holding a valid Canadian
Private or Commercial Airplane licence. You must not have flown
for hire or reward, and must not have received, or be in the process
of receiving, flight training from the Canadian Armed Forces at any
time during the previous five years (excluding Air Cadets).

Upon entering, candidates must complete a flight test with a
regional examiner. This flight test is similar to a private pilot flight
test, and usually lasts between sixty and ninety minutes. The top
candidate in each region is then selected for the final competition,
which is held in a different city each year. At the finals, candidates
undergo two separate flight tests. The first test focuses on upper-air
work; the second includes navigation and exercises covering various
phases of pilot skill. The finals also include a flight-planning exercise
as well as a practical, written examination.

Entering the competition costs $100, and you must supply your own plane (renting your plane from a flight school is the easiest option). If you make it to the finals, Air Canada provides transportation to and from the competition, as well as full accommodations while participating. Although entering the competition may cost you a bit of money, even if you don't win you have the opportunity to fly with an experienced flight instructor and test your skills. Any type of success in this competition will also look great on a résumé.

More information can be found at:
http://webstertrophycompetition.netfirms.com/

CHAPTER SIX: GETTING THE JOB

Pilots track their lives by the number of hours in the air, as if any other kind of time isn't worth noting.

—Michael Parfit, 'The Corn was
Two Feet Below the Wheels,'
Smithsonian Magazine, May 2000

S O, you've worked hard, built your hours, passed your written exam and flight test, and received your commercial licence. Now what? Getting a first job in any industry is difficult, and the aviation industry is no different. In most industries, the problem faced by newcomers is that companies want experienced employees, and yet the only way to get experience is to be hired! The problem is exacerbated in the aviation industry since pilots are judged by the amount of hours they have. Often, airlines (or their insurance company) will require that a pilot have a minimum number of hours. Therefore, if you don't have the specified number of hours, you're out of luck. In my opinion, this is a big problem in the industry. Instead, they should better regulate themselves and work on developing a paid apprenticeship program. You'll have to work hard to find your first job. Even with a degree or diploma, and despite what your flight school may say, except in rare circumstances you will not walk into a regional airline flying job right after finishing your licence.

There *are* jobs out there, and new pilots in Canada typically land their first job in one of the following ways: they work as instructors, they work the ramp of a small northern airline, they work the dock for a small northern float airline, or they work for an aviation company that specializes in things such as sightseeing, skydiving, glider towing, or aerial photography. Most are not dream jobs, and most do not pay well, but all will offer different types of experience that will be invaluable to a new pilot. Most importantly, all will eventually get you hours.

Instructing

One the most common first jobs for new pilots in Canada is to become an instructor. You've just spent 200+ hours on small trainers. Who better to teach new pilots than someone who just experienced training? Instructing can be a very rewarding job, especially for people who have the knack for teaching. Working one-on-one with a student to help them achieve their licences can be an enjoyable challenge.

In order to become an instructor, you first need to obtain an instructor rating. Yes, more training! An instructor rating can be added to your commercial licence. Similar to commercial and private training, you are required to have ground school and in-flight lessons. You're also required to come up with lesson plans and explain how you would teach a particular lesson. Lessons for becoming an instructor are different from other flight lessons. Instead of sitting in the left seat, in front of all the controls and instruments, you'll be sitting in the right seat. This will allow your student easy access to the instruments and controls. Instructor rating lessons are different in another way as well: when you are an instructor, you will be responsible for dealing with any unforeseen problems or dangerous situations. Therefore, when doing your instructor rating training, you are trained to deal with these situations. It will often be the senior instructor training you for your instructor rating that will put you into these difficult situations to see how you recover!

Becoming an instructor can have its benefits: besides the rewarding feeling of teaching, instructing can also offer you the chance to remain close to home, improve your flying skills, and get yourself flying right away. The other routes for landing a first job in

Canada typically involve moving up north and working with an airline in a remote area. For many people, especially those with a family, this is not a viable option. Many flight schools are located near large towns or cities, so as an instructor, there is a better chance that you'll be able to stay close to home. Flying can be tough on families, so getting a job that doesn't require uprooting your family is a good thing. Just keep in mind there is a good chance that at some point, you'll have to move away from your hometown for a flying job.

If you've ever done any teaching or tutoring, you'll know that one of the biggest benefits in this type of work is that it forces you to really know your stuff. Being an instructor gives you an opportunity to become extremely knowledgeable in many aviation areas such as flight basics, navigation techniques, and air regulations. Students can come up with some pretty tricky questions, and as their paid instructor, it's your duty to be able to give them answers. If you don't know the answer, it's your duty to find out. This often requires searching through the CARS or Airman's Information Manual (AIM), causing you to learn even more information as you go.

One of the other benefits of instructing is that it allows you a better chance of flying immediately. Jobs with northern airlines often require working the ramp for a certain amount of time. This can be mind-numbing work and can cause your flying skills to deteriorate. With instructing, there's the potential to start your instructor rating right after you finish your commercial licence, and depending on the school, to start instructing soon after completing your instructor rating. Deciding where to complete your instructor rating can be complicated. There are advantages for each school. Depending on the movement in the industry and the size of the school, some may be able to offer you a position before or during your actual instructor rating. Knowing there's a job waiting for you makes paying for the training much easier to swallow. Try to find a school that has more potential instructor jobs available than candidates that are being trained. For example, if a school generally only hires one or two instructors a year but currently has ten students working on their instructor rating, it is not likely that you will be hired directly after completing your training. Although an instructor rating qualifies you to instruct at any flight school, most flight schools tend to hire instructors who completed their instructor rating course at that particular school. At a very small school, there might not be any positions for you when you've completed your rating. Some schools, for example, only have two or three instructors. If none of these instructors plan to leave, it's unlikely the school can justify the hiring of another instructor, unless the number of students increases.

There are some downsides to instructing. The first is the job itself. If you're not the type of person who enjoys teaching, instructing is not for you. Students can be very frustrating to work with at times, and you need to enjoy that type of challenge. As stated earlier, students can ask some pretty tough questions—they can also ask some pretty stupid ones. Will that bother you or will you merely shrug it off? In the plane, students can also go out of their way to try to crash. One of your main responsibilities as an instructor is to allow your students to learn from their mistakes. This will often involve potentially dangerous situations, and some people are not suited to such a stressful job.

One of the other problems with the job is that, although you're building up hours, you actually fly very little yourself. You're mostly sitting in the passenger seat making sure that the student does things properly. Some people might argue that this will prepare you for a career in the airlines, where much of your time flying will actually be spent checking instruments while autopilot does the rest. This early in your career, though, you'll benefit from hands-on experience.

Another downside to instructing is the low pay. Instructors are generally required to remain at the airport in case a student walks in off the street for an intro lesson. The problem with this is that instructors are only paid for the lessons they teach. If you're there all day waiting and no students show up, you get nothing. In the summer, when flight schools are at their busiest, this is usually not a problem. In the winter, though, customers are hard to find, and money can get tight. During the slow months, most new instructors have to work another job to enjoy a guaranteed income. I knew a full-time instructor who once had a February when he earned just $95!

Hours are the main measure of a pilot's experience, but just as important is how and where those hours were acquired—complexity and speed of aircraft, for instance, are taken into consideration. For example, if you were to have 5000 hours instructing on single-engine trainers, you would be less qualified for most jobs than someone who has 2000 hours on multi-engine turboprops. So unless you want to have a career as an instructor, at some point you'll need to move on to another job. While you're instructing, it may be possible for you to have access to some multi-engine planes (if your school has one). However, it's usually the more senior instructors who are given access to the multi-engine planes, and opportunities for junior instructors will probably be limited. With the flight experience you gain from instructing, it's possible that you may be able to go directly into a co-pilot spot and skip working on the ramp, but it's still likely that you'll be required to move to a smaller town to achieve this. Even in the small town there are no guarantees that you can skip working the ramp. Therefore, even if you elect to instruct in a big city as your first job, there is still a good chance that you'll have to move to a remote location to gain experience.

Some northern operators tend to give little value to instructor time, and I've even heard of a few that will not hire former instructors. However, there are many airlines that value instructor time, and as long as it's mixed with time on larger and more complex aircraft, these airlines will look on you favourably.

Working the Ramp

The second most common beginning aviation job in Canada is working the ramp. This is a strange phenomenon not often seen in other professions. Working the ramp means working a non-flying job for the airline until a flying spot becomes available. At first, this seems counter-intuitive. Why would airlines employ a highly trained pilot to work a manual labour job? The short answer: because they can. The longer answer is more complex.

The practice of having highly trained pilots work the ramp has become a common phenomenon at smaller Canadian airlines for a number of reasons. Currently, there are far more low-time pilots than jobs. This is because insurance requirements for many airlines have increased because of the escalating legal costs of aviation mishaps. Insurance companies require their pilots to have more experience to operate most types of aircraft. As a result, the number of positions where they can use inexperienced pilots decreases. Airlines therefore have the luxury of building up a pool of trained entry-level pilots, while at the same time filling important jobs. This is especially true for airlines in remote areas. If such an airline needs a pilot at short notice, it's much easier for them to hire a pilot already based and settled in the city.

Working the ramp can take many forms, and each airline does it in their own way. Some airlines will have an unofficial list of pilots, and will use seniority as a determining factor in filling flying spots. Other airlines will have a less formal system, and fill positions more randomly. Each location will have a typical average waiting time that can vary dramatically, depending on the industry. Over the past decade, I've heard estimations of anywhere between one month and two years as the time spent working in a non-flying position before getting a flying spot. Some companies will split your duties and have you fly part-time and work a ground job part-time. It's tough to predict an exact time that one will have to wait on the ramp. However, talking to current pilots working the ramp will give you an idea of what to expect.

There are a number of different jobs that constitute working the ramp, and they vary within each airline. Ramp jobs can consist of loading and unloading luggage and cargo, grooming, driving a courtesy shuttle, customer service, and dispatch and office work. Some jobs are more pleasant than others, but the main point remains the same: work hard. Working the ramp can be challenging since you'll be observed constantly. It's essentially a never-ending job interview for a flying spot, and not a particularly fun position to be in. You've just spent a couple of years and lots of money getting a commercial pilot licence, and now here you are, living far away from home, doing a manual labour job for very little money. It can be frustrating. The rewards are worth it, though. Although it may take a while, once you start flying, you'll be quickly gaining valuable hours.

Hours spent in an actual airline environment, whether as a co-pilot on a more complex aircraft or as a Captain on a single-engine Cessna, are generally considered more valuable than hours spent instructing. Instead of just dealing with students in fair weather conditions, you have to deal with passengers, cargo, clients, your company management, and ever-changing weather conditions. You'll face similar challenges at larger airlines.

Although the starting pay on the ramp is quite low, it picks up much quicker than if you're instructing. As you gain experience, you can move up to different types of planes and gain different types of experience, which in turn makes you more valuable in the industry. It's often a slow wait on the ramp, but once you get flying, the career progression is generally a lot quicker than if you went the instructing route. The experience you get in addition to flying is also invaluable. Moving to a different town, often in remote parts of the country where most Canadians have never visited, is an exciting opportunity. It puts a completely different perspective on things. I have many great memories of my time living up north. And when you start flying, you'll have the opportunity to see some amazing sights. I've seen some beautiful scenery, witnessed spectacular displays of Northern Lights, crossed the Arctic Circle, and met tons of interesting people.

Not everyone who is hired for the ramp will be given a flying spot. Having pilot candidates work the ramp is a way for companies to see what individuals are like. When you become a pilot, the company is trusting you to take care of their aircraft, which are extremely expensive pieces of machinery! That's a lot of responsibility. If you're careless, lazy, or have a bad attitude while working the ramp, why would they trust you to take good care of their aircraft? While working the ramp, you'll also be unofficially evaluated by the other pilots. By getting your commercial licence, you've already proved you have basic flying skills, but what would you be like to work with? Cockpits, especially on the smaller turboprops, are quite cramped. You wouldn't want to sit beside someone you didn't get along with or someone who had a bad attitude. It's imperative that even when you're having a bad day, you keep a good attitude on the ramp.

There may be many pilot candidates working on the ramp, depending on the airline. In a sense, you're competing against these pilots for the next open flying position. Despite the rivalry, it's important never to go out of your way to make others look bad. If you become known as someone who's not a team player, it'll hurt your chances in getting a pilot spot. The best piece of advice for succeeding while working on the ramp is to not think of yourself as a pilot. Instead, think of yourself as someone who's working the ramp. Strive to do a good job while working on the ramp.

Working the Dock

Working the dock is similar to working the ramp, but is specific to float plane operators. Instead of loading planes from the apron, you'll be loading them from the dock. Canada has a thriving float-plane industry that is centered on remote fishing and hunting lodges in the north. Besides the inherent differences in landing a plane on water as opposed to landing on a runway, float flying in Canada is different to other types of airline operations because of the fact that very few float planes require a co-pilot. With no co-pilot required, it's tougher for newer pilots to gain experience. The unique challenges that face float pilots also mean that insurance companies will generally require higher levels of experience to fly as a Captain with passengers. As a result, many float operators require a certain amount of float time, often fifty or more hours, before you are able to fly passengers. Although you should check with specific operators' insurance companies beforehand, their idea of float hours can differ from Transport Canada's definition of float hours. For example, while Transport Canada won't count co-pilot hours in a single-engine float plane towards a higher licence, an insurance company *may* count those hours as float time or time on type.

Working the dock not only allows float operators to see what type of worker you are and how you get along with other employees, it also allows them to give you an opportunity to fly some cargo-only flights, which builds up your float hours without any passengers. Like working the ramp, working the dock can be physically demanding. It will help if you know how to swim, as there's a good chance that you'll fall in the lake at least once while loading a plane!

Most floatplane operators in Canada only operate during the summer months. Some floatplanes can be converted into ski planes to land on frozen lakes, but even still, business dramatically drops off in the winter months. Not too many people want to go north during the harsh winter months in northern Canada. Depending on movement in the industry, what will often happen is that you'll generally work the dock for one summer while getting a few hours flying cargo and then the next summer return and fly on a regular basis. Also, depending on the operator, more complex aircraft may be available. In such a case, it may be possible for you to work your way up to these planes and increase your experience.

Float flying in Canada is an exciting job. Canadian Bush pilots have numerous adventure stories. With Canada's vast wilderness and infinite number of lakes, being a bush pilot allows you an amazing opportunity to experience the Canadian Wilderness. As a float pilot, you're required to be independent and resourceful. Often, lakes that you land on are hundreds of kilometres away from the nearest settlement. Float flying also offers a greater amount of freedom than flying a conventional wheel airplane. You're no longer limited to airports and runways, and you can land in almost any lake you wish.

Float flying is not for everybody, though. You'll be spending your summers working hard in remote locations, often far away from any city. You'll generally be laid off for the winter. This can be a good thing or a bad thing, depending on your perspective. On the one hand, you don't have a year-round job; on the other hand, you have the opportunity to pursue other activities during the winter and still have a job to come back to the next summer. Some pilots work in non-aviation jobs for the winter to earn money, while others go back to school. Some even use the time to take a working vacation, spending the winter working and playing at a ski resort.

Other Routes

Becoming an instructor or working the ramp or dock are the two main ways pilots start out in Canada, but there are some other less common routes worth mentioning. Small planes are used in many different capacities, and they all need pilots. These jobs are more difficult to classify than the northern route or the instructor route. These jobs can include aerial photography, towing gliders for the air cadets or a gliding club, flying skydivers, aerial sightseeing flights, pipeline patrol, and even flying for a family friend or relative. With these jobs, as well as with many other flying jobs, it's often a case of knowing the right people and being at the right place at the right time.

While the more advanced aerial photography often requires complex aircraft and equipment, there's a small market for personalized aerial photography services. Farmers, developers, and numerous other parties often need aerial pictures of their properties. There are a number of companies that have utilized small aircraft for just this purpose. This can be a great way to accumulate flying time during the summer months. Pilots who choose this option may also afford themselves a wonderful opportunity to see the country, since their base airport can often change on a regular basis.

Separate from aerial photography companies, some resourceful pilots have even used the aerial photography approach as a way to finance their own flying. There have been cases where pilots have rented an aircraft and taken aerial pictures of homes or businesses, and then attempted to sell these pictures to the property owners. Success is not guaranteed, but it sounds like a potentially great way to ease the high costs associated with flying.

Flying gliders and skydivers can be a good way to build hours and perfect your take-off and landing techniques. There are a number of skydive operators located throughout the country, and they need pilots to fly the skydivers. Flying Skydivers can be monotonous, though. You climb up to a certain altitude, have the jumpers jump out, and then you descend as quickly as possible to pick up more skydivers. Flying skydivers usually does not pay very well and is often as low as $1 per jumper. Pilots can make more money rolling up parachutes than they can flying the jumpers! Do make sure you get paid, by the way. Skydiving companies exist to make a profit, and as a pilot, you deserve to be paid for your services. This can be a problem, as you'll see in the "Working For Free" section. The majority of skydiving takes place on the weekends, and so pilots will often spend their weekend at the jump zone, camping out and barbecuing dinner. The pay is not great, but it can be a wonderful way to spend a summer—you'll build up your hours, too!

There are also numerous gliding clubs located across the country. Gliders need a powered airplane to tow them up to altitude so that they can glide back to earth. Most gliding clubs are non-profit, and therefore pilots are not paid for their services. Because of the gliding clubs' non-profit status, many of them do not even require you to have a commercial pilot's licence. This means that even if you only have your private licence, it's a viable option for accumulating hours. While you wouldn't get paid, being part of the club could give you the opportunity to obtain your glider pilot licence over a summer while flying. As an aside, you can count fifty hours of glider flight time towards your Airline Transport Licence. Towing gliders can be a good way accumulate hours, however, like flying skydivers, the flying can be relatively monotonous. Although having a couple hundred hours towing gliders will help your chances in getting a job, having too much time towing gliders will actually hinder your chances.

If you're a member of the Air Cadets, there's an opportunity to tow gliders and give familiarization flights through their organization. The position can be tough to get, but once obtained, can pay quite well for a summer's work, and can be lots of fun. As with flying at gliding clubs, the job can become monotonous after a while. Completing too many familiarization flights can also negatively affect your career, so if you pursue this avenue, keep it in moderation.

Towing gliders is generally done on tail-wheel aircraft. This is when the wheel that does most of the ground steering is located at the tail of the aircraft, and not the front. Almost all modern airliners have a nose wheel, whereas most older planes have a tail wheel. In today's world, it can be difficult to gain tail-wheel experience, and most clubs require at least five hours. There are a small number of flying schools that have tail-wheel aircraft on which they can instruct. Ask your local gliding club if they know of any schools nearby.

Flying sightseers, doing pipeline patrol, and flying traffic patrols are also other jobs that often do not require a high number of hours. With sightseeing, although you're flying passengers, it's generally only in good weather and not far from your departure airport. With pipeline patrols, you fly above a gas or oil pipeline and make sure there are no leaks or potential threats to the pipeline. In some cities, radio stations have traffic reporters that broadcast from small planes, and they require a pilot. Depending on the radio station, they may or may not have their own plane and pilot. If not, they will often contract a freelance pilot from a local flight school. These kinds of jobs can be a great way to gain hours.

Finding a Job

Aviation Companies, especially the smaller operators who hire low-time pilots, are spread across the country. You can expect to move at some point in your career. As previously mentioned, it may be easier to find an instructor's job closer to home. In contrast, it can be extremely difficult to find a ramp or charter job in a big city as a low-time pilot.

The time to start looking for an instructor position is when you're completing your commercial licence. Attempt to get to know both your instructor and the Chief Flight Instructor at the school where you train. Also notice how many instructors are at the school and what the movement is. You should be able to get a good idea of how likely you are to be hired by a school after you complete your flight instructor rating training with them. If the chances appear slim, it might be advantageous to look around to other flight schools. Depending on the movement in the industry, some are often desperate for instructors, while others may need extra instructors for the busy season. While a permanent job may be better than a seasonal job, a seasonal job is better than no job, and will put you in a position where you're gaining hours.

There are four classes of instructors. When you first receive your instructor's rating, you become a class IV instructor. You will now require supervision from a class I or II instructor while completing the rest of your training. For example, a class I instructor may have to go for a quick flight with your student before you're allowed to give them permission to go solo. To go from a class IV to a class III instructor, you need to give at least three recommends for students to take their Private Pilot Licence Flight test. Once you're a class III instructor, you're no longer under the direct supervision of a class I instructor and are able to work more independently.

When the Air Cadets complete their summer program to obtain their private pilot licence, the government will contract various flight schools to provide the training over the summer. One of the best ways to get an instructing job is to find one of these schools that have a contract to train air cadets. Plan to complete your instructor rating mid-spring, and then, hopefully, you will be hired to instruct air cadets over the summer (schools always need more instructors during the summer months). Although it may only be a summer position, it will get you more hours, give you the opportunity to get the necessary recommendations for a flight test, and allow you to move up from a class IV to a class III instructor. This will make you more employable elsewhere, too.

Finding a job on the ramp or the dock can be more difficult than finding an instructor's job. This is primarily because most small airlines are based in smaller, more remote communities. Some are even located where the only way in or out is by plane! Wings Magazine (http://www.wingsmagazine.com/) publishes an annual list of charter and scheduled airlines in Canada (as well as flight schools). Pilot Career Centre (http://www.pilotcareercentre.com/) also has a list of various operators, along with their addresses, and often their minimum hiring requirements. Both of these databases are invaluable in figuring out where to focus your job search.

While completing your training (and following completion), it's a good idea to keep in touch with other students. And not just students who're at your own level—keep in touch with students who are ahead of you as well. Seeing where they get jobs will help you to better focus your search and can even give you an "in" with a particular operator. In most industries, the normal way to get a job is to send in a résumé, and if they're interested in you, they'll call you back to arrange an interview. This is generally not the way it works in aviation. Companies get hundreds of résumés each year from low-time pilots, and you're therefore unlikely to hear back from them if you take this approach. Sending in a résumé is not a bad idea to get your name into the company's system, but unless you know someone at the company who's putting in a good word for you, it may be necessary to go up and introduce yourself.

For companies located outside your immediate area, there are two steps to this process: going on a road trip, and then "lurking." The road trip is a long-established tradition for young pilots, and involves getting in your car, driving to all the remotely located airlines, and dropping off your résumé with the Chief Pilot. Road trips are most commonly done in the spring and early summer, but they can be done anytime of the year. If you're attempting to get a job flying floats, then going on a road trip in the winter is pretty pointless, since most of the operators are not yet open. Summer road trips are less expensive, since you can cut down the costs by camping along the way. Print off a bunch of résumés and make a list of all the operators you want to go visit. Try to learn the name of the Chief Pilot at the airline you're applying to and address the cover letter and résumé accordingly.

When you're applying for jobs, it's best to target a smaller number of companies and make a concerted effort to find information on them. Be diligent not just in sending out your résumé, but also in following up and trying to arrange a time to meet the person responsible for hiring. Merely sending out a "cookie cutter" résumé and cover letter will not impress anyone.

Hangar Talk – Finding a Job

My first job in aviation was as a cargo handler for Skyward Aviation in Thompson, which I found through a friend of mine in flight school. I did that for 27 months and then was promoted to a Medevac First Officer on a C441 and C421.
—Andy Gould, Metroliner First Officer – Perimeter Aviation

My first job was First officer on Grand Commander and Merlin for domestic charters and IFR multi-engine simulator instructor. The company I was training with was short of pilots. I started work the day after I got my IFR (right place at the right time, pure luck).
—Chris Knox, A340/A330 Captain – Air Canada

It's really hard to get your first job—you basically can either head north or instruct. It's unlikely you'll be on a Dash-8 or a Lear jet right after graduation, and most schools give new pilots an unrealistic idea of what their first few years in aviation will be like. My first job was as a dispatcher then First Officer and then Captain for Northern Dene Airways in Stoney Rapids, Saskatchewan. The Ops manager went to the same flight college I did, and he decided to give me a chance.
—Shane Murphy, Corporate C550 Captain

My first real job was flying a C206 and C207 out of Inuvik NWT. I was working as a co-operative student engineer at Canadian Airlines. My direct supervisor was also a commercial pilot, and he had taken

the last two summers off to go and fly in Inuvik NWT as well. He told me about the company... I contacted them and got lucky. Got hired over the phone and was flying the first day I got there.
  —*Geoff Cattrall, A340/A330 Second Officer – Cathay Pacific*

To help you find your first job, work in the industry, network wherever possible, and follow up on all leads and contacts available. You never know who may help you get your first job. Educate yourself, follow industry news, read forums and magazines, and know what's going on where. Target a small number of companies and work hard at it instead of sending a bulk e-mail to 300 carriers. At the same time, don't assume any door is shut. Don't be afraid to travel and get your face out there. My first job was as a medevac F/O on a C414, which I'd heard about through word-of-mouth.
  —*Greg McMaster, Convair CV 580 Tanker First Officer—ConAir*

Detective Work

Finding information about small airlines can be quite difficult. The databases listed earlier, along with the airline websites, are a good starting point for finding out information. Take notes on all the information that you can find. Most important is to know the name and proper spelling of the person responsible for hiring—usually the Chief Pilot. Learning about the airline itself (their fleet, their routes, their history, and their minimum hiring requirements), will also be very helpful. It's extremely beneficial if you know someone who works for the company, but if you don't know anyone there are still ways in. Although it is extremely beneficial if you know someone working for the company, if you do not, it may not be a bad idea to call and try and talk to someone, not necessarily the Chief Pilot, to find out what the hiring process is like or any particular questions you have about the operation. Be sure that you are extremely polite to whomever you are speaking with. Even if they are just a receptionist, they could be someone that the Chief Pilot trusts and they may be very helpful. If they seem busy or annoyed that you called, try to remain as polite as possible, but don't pester them.

The best-case scenario for submitting a résumé is to have a current employee pass it on to the Chief Pilot for you. As mentioned in the networking section, this can be a difficult task, but the benefits can be well worth the effort.

When you start the application process, make a chart, take notes, and keep track of the information that you find. Have the airline, its contact information, its fleet information, its hiring information, and your progress with the applications all in one easy-to-read format. Keep track of when you sent in a résumé, when you called, when you followed up, and who you spoke with. The challenge is to talk to them enough so that you become familiar to them (don't overdo it, though. You don't want to pester them). If you give a quick e-mail, phone call, or visit every month or so, you should be all right.

You should be starting your detective work as early as possible. As I mentioned in an earlier chapter, you should be attempting to meet people from the very beginning—as soon as you begin your training.

Aviation Résumés

Although simply sending a résumé to an airline is unlikely to get you your first job, it's nonetheless one of the most important tools for presenting yourself to an airline. During my research for this book, I spoke with former Chief Pilots Greg McMaster of Skyward Aviation, Marc Paille of Skylink Express and Shane Murphy of Western Aviation to discover what potential pilots should include on their résumé. The overwhelming response from these Chief Pilots (and other industry insiders who are in charge of hiring), is that if there are significant spelling errors or the Chief Pilot's name is spelled wrong, they'll file that candidate's résumé in the garbage.

These are some examples of actual mistakes made on résumés. I'm not including them to suggest that these people are unintelligent, but rather to show how easy it is to overlook simple grammatical errors, and what a devastating impact they can have on your chances of being hired.

"I am a perfessional pilot"

—How Perrrfect.

"I would very much lik the chanse to meet you in to discuss my application"
　　—What's a chanse and why are you going to lik it?

"I have lived in Saudy Arabia for the past 3 1/2 years. I enjoy Soudy Arabia but would like to come back to Canada"
　　—I'm sure the Soudie's will be glad to hear you enjoy their country.

"I have a great attentions to detail"
　　—Sure you do.

"I hop to talk to you soon about future employment with your company."
　　—Are you a kangaroo?

"I shall be very grateful and hard wroking."
　　—Awesome dude! Someone who will wrok hard! Perhaps we can rewire the aircraft for electric guitar plugins.

"As a Chef Pilot I have a strong background in working with operations related materials and records."
　　—Mmmmmm, chef pilot. If this was actually true, this person would have a definite advantage in their candidacy—anyone who can prepare delicious in-flight meals would be great company on long trips.

　　Chief Pilots have résumés sent to them everyday, and if it's for an entry-level position, there are likely hundreds of qualified candidates for only a limited number of positions. Why give them the opportunity to throw your application in the garbage because of a simple spelling error? Before sending out your résumé, have someone you know look over your résumé for any spelling or grammatical errors, and make sure you use the spell-check feature on your word processing software.

　　The most important item on an aviation résumé is flight time. Even if you have a low number of hours, Chief Pilots want to see it stand out in an-easy-to-read format such as a table. Don't make them dig for it. Be sure to give them total time (TT), P.I.C. time, and if applicable, multi-engine time, turbine time, float time, and time on any aircraft that the airline operates. When stating your hours, be sure to round to the nearest five or ten hours and DON'T include a decimal place. I know that when you only have 213.5 hours that the extra 0.5 makes a huge difference to you, but Chief Pilots really don't care, and to them, it looks silly and makes your résumé harder to read. It's much easier to simply put 215 hours, or if you want to be on the safe side, round down to 210 hours. In the long run, someone with 213.7 hours is not going to get hired over someone with 213.2 hours simply because they have 0.5 hours more experience. That being said, there are certain hour marks that do make a difference. For example, 1000 hours is a bit of a magic number in the industry, and this is a requirement to fly certain types of aircraft. So never round up to 1000 hours if you have not exceeded that amount of time.

The overall format of your résumé is also important. Start with the basics. Although it may seem to be an attention-grabber, don't use fancy-coloured résumé paper and DON'T attach a picture of yourself standing in front of the first plane you soloed in. Too many pilots send out their résumé on cloud-coloured paper with a big picture of themselves front and center—this is so cliché, and I haven't met a single Chief Pilot who would hire someone with that type of résumé. It's probably the quickest way (even quicker than spelling mistakes) to get your résumé tossed in the trash. Paper should be white or slightly off-white, and of good quality. An aviation résumé should be a maximum of two pages, but keeping it down to one page is ideal. The format should be easy to read with flight time, experience, and licences all front and center, and it should be printed in black ink. Although small dashes of colour may nicely highlight the important information in your résumé, too much colour will make it difficult to read.

Things to make sure you include:

Contact Information: make sure this is up to date. Pilots who are often on the road should ensure the contact phone number is a cell number. If you insist on putting your home phone number, make sure you have someone who sounds professional to take your messages. If you move or your contact information changes, you have a perfect excuse to send in a new résumé.

Flight Time: I can't stress this enough. Chief Pilots DO NOT want to have to search for your times. Don't hide them obscurely in the middle of your résumé, and don't place them timidly in the middle of your cover letter. Make sure they stand out and demand attention at first glance, and in a format that is easy to review and understand.

Licences, Ratings & Qualifications: These should be easy to find and placed on either side of your flight times. Chief Pilots are busy, and similar to the flight times, they do not want to search for what ratings you possess. You don't necessarily have to put that you have a class I medical certificate, since it's assumed that you already have one. However, if you have any extreme restrictions, such as "day flight only," or "can only fly with another crew member," it might be a good idea to include it. It'll decrease your chances of finding employment, but at least you're being honest. If you do have these restrictions, you're going to be very limited in your flying career.

Types of Aircraft Flown: This information is also of great importance, especially if you've flown any of the aircraft types that the airline you're applying to has in their fleet. Do not list every single variation of the aircraft types that you've flown. For example, if you've flown a Cessna 172S and a Cessna 172R, do not put both of them. You may think that it's making you look more experienced, but it's unnecessary information (or overkill) and is therefore not impressing anybody.

Education: Education is not as important to potential employers as flight times and aircraft type flown, but it's still information you must include. Make sure to specify any significant training you've undergone, such as an aviation college diploma or a university degree. Even if you completed your flight training at a local flying club, be sure to mention it. If you have a university degree, make a note of the university where you studied (elementary school and high school details are unnecessary).

Work Experience: In this section, Chief Pilots are mostly looking for aviation-related work experience. Even if you haven't had a flying position before, if you've worked in an aviation related job, be sure to include it. But you ask, "What if you haven't had an aviation related job before?" In that case, put down the more important non-aviation related jobs you've worked at, and especially the ones you held down for a long time. While this won't get you points in the *prior experience* category, it will at least let the airline know that you've been in the working world before and have held down a job for a significant period of time.

Other Interests: There's some debate as to whether pilots should include this section in their résumés. On one hand, there's a lot of extra information that's not relevant to how you'll perform as a pilot. As Greg McMaster, former Chief Pilot of Skyward Aviation mentions "I don't care about your volunteer work experience during recess in grade 6." On the other hand, however, some interests may make you more employable or more apt to stay at that particular airline for a long time. For example, if you have experience driving a forklift, loading any type of cargo, and general maintenance, those are skills that could prove useful for a northern operator. However, if you're applying to a northern operator and your interests and hobbies include sun tanning, shopping, and eating at fancy restaurants, you may want to leave that information off. Although those are extreme examples, you'll have to decide for yourself if the information is relevant for the job you're applying for.

References: Be sure to include references in your résumé with names, addresses, and phone numbers. If possible, try to include an internal reference who works for the company, or somebody the Chief Pilot knows. Failing that, try to include either a past instructor, teacher, or employer who can provide a reference. Don't just include a friend. Be sure to ask your references if you can mention them in your résumé.

In the references section, do not put "references available on request." Chief Pilots don't want to have to go on some sort of scavenger hunt to find out who your references are. Except in very rare circumstances, they'll not call you to request a list of your references. They will simply look to another candidate who was kind enough to include this information on his or her résumé.

Goal: I've heard differing opinions on whether or not to put your employment goals on an aviation résumé. I think it depends on the operation. Is there any doubt as to what you're applying for? Are there different positions that you may be eligible for, or is there only one spot? If you're applying to a smaller operator that only hires pilots for flying positions, putting that your goal is to be a pilot is redundant. However, if you're applying to an operator that will hire people onto the dock or ramp prior to flying, mentioning that you are looking for employment that will eventually lead to a flying position may not be a bad idea. It may seem obvious that your goal is to one day secure a flying position, but it's still worth making it clear. You don't want to find yourself in a job where your boss thinks you're happy loading cargo for the rest of your life!

Personal Information: I generally would not put this information on a résumé. For the most part, it doesn't matter, it takes up space, and it will not help you in securing a job. For example, an employer generally doesn't care if you're married or how tall you are. However, there may be times when it's prudent to mention personal details. A willingness to relocate, for example, may be something a potential employer would be interested to hear.

Padding your Logbook

It can be disheartening and frustrating when you're first starting out. Your hour totals are low, you haven't flown many types of aircraft, and you don't have much work experience. One of the biggest mistakes new pilots make is to try to fill their résumé. They add things that have no relevance to getting a flying job. You might think it helps to make you look like a well-rounded individual, but for the most part, too much fill just annoys a Chief Pilot. As previously noted, it's fine to mention some non-aviation information, but do so sparingly and only when relevant.

This should go without saying, but it's worth a reminder: Never pad your log book with false claims or state that you've flown more hours than you actually have. You'll get caught! It's quite easy to tell if someone's falsified their log book or added hours to their résumé. This will have terrible results for your career and possibly for the safety of your passengers. A logbook is a legal document, and it's illegal to claim hours you've not flown. Falsifying your logbook could have dire consequences. The aviation community is a small, tight-knit one, and if you're discovered to have falsified your logbook you will never repair the damage done to your reputation. It's simply not worth it, so don't do it!

Cover Letters

For initial jobs in aviation, a cover letter is less important than a résumé, but including one can help sum up your application. As with résumés, make sure that your spelling is correct and addressed to the correct person. Don't use a generic "Dear Sir or Madam" or "To whom it may concern." Cover letters should be polite and to the point. In the cover letter, it's important not to appear desperate. Do not say that you'll fly for free (more on that later), or pay for training, or work for less than the usual wage. These offers not only make you appear desperate, but they also tell potential employers that you have issues with self-respect and dignity. You may think you're making yourself more competitive in showing your willingness to work hard, but there's a line that should not be crossed.

Following Up

After you've sent in a résumé, it's a good idea to follow up with a phone call, an e-mail, or a visit (or possibly all three). The goal is to have the Chief Pilot *know of* you, but not be *sick of* you. If a suitable position becomes available, you want the Chief Pilot to think of you as one of the candidates. For the most part, this means stopping by for a visit just to say hello. For the smaller northern operators, this means going on a road trip. For other operators, it means calling ahead and trying to schedule a time to meet with the Chief Pilot.

The road trip, while decreasing in popularity since 2001, is still a good way to get out and meet some of the more remote operators so they can put a face with the name. It can be tricky to plan a trip that doesn't take up too much time, and yet still allows you an opportunity to see the required operators. Try to call ahead in most instances, and ask if the Chief Pilot will be around and, if so, when it would be a convenient time to stop by. Some operators don't mind if you show up unannounced; they appreciate that you went out of your way to show an interest. Operators with this attitude will be happy to give you five minutes of their time, even if there are currently no positions available. However, there are other operators who can't stand people who show up unannounced. On your road trip, bring camping equipment, work clothes, and all your flying gear.

You never know when you might hit the jackpot and land a job unexpectedly.

Getting lucky is the exception, not the norm, and despite knowing of a few pilots who found a job this way, it's much more likely that your road trip will end without landing a new job. Even if this is the case, your road trip will have achieved something important—you will have met many Chief Pilots, made a good impression on them, and when a position becomes available they'll be more inclined to offer it to you.

Lurking

One other tactic to make yourself more competitive is the process known as *lurking*. Lurking involves targeting a small number of operators in a single town and relocating nearby. During slow times in the industry, this becomes more common. Although moving to an unfamiliar town without a job doesn't seem like a pleasant idea, you'll make yourself much more competitive for a job. As is often the case for small airlines, someone will leave suddenly or circumstances will change, and they'll need someone right away. They don't want to hire someone living on the other side of the country because that will take too long. They'll like the fact that you're nearby and can start work as soon as the next day. The towns generally targeted for lurking are ones that have a few different operators that hire low-time pilots, the most popular of which are Yellowknife, Fort McMurray, Prince Albert, Thompson, and Red Lake. Moving to one of these towns will not guarantee a job, but it does show your determination to get a job with that airline. As long as you're polite, persistent, and social, there's a good chance that it'll lead to a job. That being said, you should have an ejection plan. Decide how long you're going to stay in that town before you give up. If you're in town for too long and start getting bitter about not getting hired, this attitude will just decrease your chances of being hired.

When I first relocated to Thompson, a number of my friends and classmates thought I was crazy. Why would I move all the way up there without a job? In my case, I was lucky in that I already knew a few people in town, but it was still a difficult thing to do. Eighteen months later, when I was flying as a First Officer on Medevacs, those people who had doubted my decision to move were now asking me to put in a good word for them at my airline!

Interviews

For larger airlines, the interview process is significantly more standardized, and I'll discuss that in Chapter 9. At the entry level, interviews can vary greatly between operators. So although it's frustrating, you really have to be prepared for anything. Most importantly, do your homework. This shouldn't be a problem for you if you've already done your detective work. Before you go for your interview or stop by to say hello, review your notes on that particular operator. One of the things you should try to find out is what to wear when going for an interview with a northern operator. Although different companies will have different corporate cultures, in general, plan on business/casual attire. A suit is unnecessary, but clean shoes, pressed khakis or slacks, and a nice button-up shirt or golf shirt are recommended. For women, the same type of dress code applies, but go easy on the makeup, jewellery, and perfume. You should always have a change of work clothes and a set of work gloves in your car, so that you're ready to go if an operator wants you to start right away.

If possible, go on interviews and road trips alone. Here's a story told to me by Greg McMaster: On one occasion, three acquaintances were applying for the same job at the same time, but with separate interviews. They were asked the same question: Why should I hire you over your friends? The applicant who had the best things to say about their friends got the job. The remaining applicants, on the other hand, all lost out because they were prepared to bad-mouth the others to improve their own chances. Don't put other people down to make yourself look better. That includes both people that are there with you, and other people you've met or worked with. If you're the type that would so eagerly speak ill of people in front of a complete stranger, what does that say about your character?

One of the biggest mistakes new pilots make during the interview process is not being prepared. You don't need to go so far as to memorize every single answer, but after going on a few interviews, you'll begin to notice that the same questions are asked again and again. This is especially true of introductory questions.

Interviewers will want to know about your background, education, previous jobs, and perhaps career goals. Think about these answers beforehand and have an idea of what you're going to say. What's an interviewer going to think if they ask, "So, tell me about yourself," and you have nothing to say? This is your opportunity to tell them about yourself, so use it. You don't often get an opportunity to call up a Chief Pilot and tell them how great you are. Don't sound too cocky, but be confident in your delivery.

Some of the questions to expect are, "What do you know about this company?" and "Why do you want to work here?" Have some prepared responses for this kind of question. It can be tough, because in many situations you'll just want to say, "Well, I want to work here because you have airplanes and I want to get paid to fly them." Instead, try to think of a couple of reasons as to why you'd want to work for that particular operator. You don't have to go overboard and say that flying an old Piper Navajo located in Fort-Middle-Of-Nowhere is your dream job and you want to retire there. Just focus on some of the reasons why this particular company was on your short list. While the location might not be the greatest, it might be better than other spots, and maybe you've got friends or family there. Maybe they have a particular plane in their fleet that you want to fly or they have a certain set of destinations that you want to go to. Most Chief Pilots of small northern operators know that this job is just a time-building step for you and that you don't want to be there for the rest of your life. But they don't want a pilot who'll leave town at the earliest possible chance either. Be honest about it, and if the town is a place you could see yourself living for a few years, let them know.

You also have to make sure that you're up-to-date with your general flying regulations. You should have some basic knowledge, and the Chief Pilot may ask questions that were similar to some of the oral questions that were asked on your commercial flight test or during your instrument rating flight test. You're not expected to know every single answer, but you should know most of them. Sometimes the interviewer will simply ask you questions to see how you think. For example, Marc Paille, former Chief Pilot of Skylink Express, would often ask candidates what they would do if they had a particular emergency or situation. While he was obviously hoping the candidates would offer him the correct procedures, he was also looking at the candidates' thought processes. Did they simply go through the procedures, or did they think things through in a logical fashion to help identify and rectify the problem?

Other times, you may just get an interviewer who wants to chat with you. At smaller operators, you become very close with your co-workers and not only have to work with them everyday, but also share a crew house and socialize with them. As a result, Chief Pilots will want to hire someone they get along with. In this situation, it really is imperative that you try to be yourself and not just say things the Chief Pilot wants to hear.

Whatever the type of interview you receive, always be sure not to speak poorly about other people or your old employer. While there may have been things that you didn't like about your old job or co-workers, these things can be stated tactfully without sounding like you're spreading gossip about your old employer. If you're bad-mouthing your old boss, the interviewer is going to assume that in no time at all, you'll be bad-mouthing him.

Overall, be honest. Some of the interview questions may be pretty tough, and if the interviewer thinks you're being dishonest or evasive, even if you gave the "right" answer, it's not going to impress them. According to Shane Murphy, candidates should avoid sucking up, but conversely, not give the impression that the job is below them. This can be a delicate balance.

Working for Free

Finding a first job can be tough. You need hours to get a job, but the best way to get hours is to get a job. It's the proverbial chicken-or-the-egg problem, and it can be very frustrating. In my opinion, however, it's very important to not think that hours are, in themselves, a form of payment. As a commercial pilot, if a company is making money from your services, you should not fly without being paid. This is different if you're flying for a charitable organization or a non-profit club. Since they're not making money, you could be seen as providing a service.

Although a number of the more shady operators have been shut down in the recent past (due to some fatal accidents), there will always be companies that will take advantage of a new pilot's desire to gain hours. They'll sell you a PPC (Pilot Proficiency Check) on one of their aircraft and then give you an opportunity to accumulate flying hours by hiring you to fly without pay. A skydiving company outside of Toronto will hold annual ground schools for a number of pilots. For just over $1,000 pilots receive a few hours on a Cessna 185, training on how to fly skydivers all under the false impression that they'll be offered employment at the end of the course. The reality is, of the dozen or so people in the course, only a couple will get hired and the rest are out of luck and have lost their $1,000. The few who are hired are not paid for flying, but they can make some money rolling up parachutes. So not only do you not get paid to fly, but there are some people who pay $1000 to get a 'course' on a 185 and don't even get the 'opportunity' to fly for free. This is a scam. While it's technically not illegal, all you'll get out of the deal is a hole in your pocket. You'd be much better off spending that $1,000 on gas for a road trip, or putting it towards an instructor rating.

Flying for free is detrimental to the individual pilot and the overall pilot profession. For the individual pilot, it can be harmful to both your chequebook and your reputation. Although you're gaining hours, you're not making any money. Hours in themselves cannot buy food. If you're lucky enough to have wealthy parents to support you, then lucky you! If you're not so fortunate, then you will likely have to work a second job. This could potentially affect your safety and the safety of your passengers. If you're working two jobs, you could potentially be skipping out on much-needed rest and flying while fatigued. There have been numerous accidents where pilot fatigue has been the main cause. Do you really want to risk your life for a job that doesn't even pay you? Flying for free can also be harmful to your reputation as a pilot. The aviation industry is generally quite small. Chief Pilots know which operators have "fly for free" schemes and many will refuse to hire anyone who has flown for free. Taking a job in which you do not get paid could essentially end up blacklisting you from airlines who do pay well.

Flying for free also hurts the pilot profession as a whole. Pilot salaries, although relatively high after a few years of experience, are actually quite low at the entry-level. Airlines are trying to make money, and employee salaries are an expense. If there are pilots willing to work for free, that is one less expense for them to worry about. Why would they pay a decent wage to someone if there's someone else willing to fly for free? This causes a problem for legitimate companies that do pay their pilots well. In order to compete, they have to find ways to reduce their expenses to match the other company that doesn't pay its pilots. This could lead to an overall reduction in salaries across the industry. I think the reasoning for some pilots who fly for free is that if they fly for free for a little while and get hours, then they'll be able to get a good job that pays well. However, if more and more pilots fly for free, there will be less and less good paying jobs available. In the long run, this will not only hurt your career prospects, but also the prospects of all the other pilots out there. I cannot stress this enough: Unless it's for a charity group or a non-profit club, DO NOT FLY FOR FREE!

Training Bonds

Training Bonds are different than flying for free, but are still relatively controversial. While most of the pilot community are quick to frown on flying for free, there are varying opinions on training bonds. Training bonds are put in place to protect the company's investment that they make in pilots during the training period, and can take a couple of different forms. The first is a promissory note from the pilot. In the note, the pilot states that if he or she leaves the company before a certain length of time (normally one to two years), they'll pay their employing company a percentage of the training costs. The second form of training bond involves the pilot paying all his training fees upfront, prior to training. The training company will then pay the pilot back a percentage of the fees each month in their paycheque. It's essentially a financial incentive to keep the pilot under their employment. Training a pilot is expensive. If a company were to have pilots leave right after being trained, they would lose a significant amount of money. It can be argued that a company should treat its employees well enough so that they do not want to leave, but there are certain circumstances, such as location and fleet, that are beyond a company's control. For most people, even if a company located in a remote northern area paid well and treated their employees with respect, they would not stay if given the opportunity to fly more advanced aircraft in a more populated area.

Training bonds are not only for the smaller operators. Some larger airlines also have bonds. The now defunct airline JetsGo required its pilots to pay a $30,000 bond prior to training. This was a perfect example of the problem with training bonds. When JetsGo shut down and declared bankruptcy, all the pilots lost their bonds. So not only were they out of a job, but they were also out a certain percentage of the $30,000. It can be a risky proposition. As long as companies are at risk of losing money because of pilots leaving shortly after their training is complete, they will continue to protect themselves financially.

It can be difficult when trying to decide whether a training bond is right for you. Some pilots will refuse to work at a company that requires a bond, while others accept that it's just a part of the industry. Paying a company a large sum of money for a training bond is a gamble. There is no guarantee that you will get it back. If you decide to get a job that requires a training bond, be sure to do your research. How is the company to work for? What are the conditions? What's the turnover rate? Why are current pilots leaving? Know what you're getting yourself into before you make a commitment.

A few other airlines will require a type rating on their specific type of aircraft before they'll hire you. You pay for the rating, unlike a bond, and the airline will not specifically pay you back on top of your regular pay. This means that you're out the cost of the training, often in the amount of tens of thousands of dollars. However, you're not committed to that specific airline for any amount of time. This could be advantageous if the aircraft type is common in Canada, but if there aren't many operators of that particular plane, then you're pretty much committed to that particular employer. This may seem cheap, but some of the most successful airlines in the US have this requirement.

Taking out a loan to get a training bond, or simply paying to buy your type rating, is a difficult venture for many entry-level pilots—many of whom are in debt from student loans. In a perfect world, training bonds would not be necessary. The companies would absorb the cost of training and pilots would stay committed to jobs long enough for the employer to recoup their training cost. This is unfortunately not the case. Aviation is a very cyclical industry, and often the movement is quick. It's likely there will always be pilots who leave a job soon after starting, and the companies therefore have to protect their training investment. It's possible to go through your career without a training bond, and some pilots will do that. If you're in a position where a job requires a training bond, look at all the information and then make an informed decision.

CHAPTER SEVEN: YOUR FIRST FLYING JOB

To most people, the sky is the limit. To those who love aviation, the sky is home.

—anonymous

S O, you have made it through your training, as well as possibly doing an instructor's rating or working the ramp and are now a full fledged pilot. Take a step back, pat yourself on the back, and congratulate yourself. You've worked hard and should be proud of yourself. When someone asks what you do, you can now say you're a pilot. It's a pretty cool feeling when you tell people what you do and they're impressed. OK, enough of that, get back to work, you've got a job to do!

Many pilots will tell you that you learn the most at your first job. Whether you're instructing, flying as a Captain on a smaller plane, or flying as a co-pilot on a slightly larger one, you'll gain an enormous amount of knowledge at your first job. It's like trying to take a drink of water from a fire hose. When you first start flying professionally, there are massive amounts of new information that you're required to know. You're now required to know your plane inside and out, know the area you'll be flying, know the company's in-flight Standard Operating Procedures (S.O.P.s), and know all of the company's ways of doing things outside of flying.

While some of your co-workers or Captains may cut you some slack because you're new, the passengers will not. The last thing a nervous flyer wants to hear is that it's the first day on the job for one of the pilots. Although the transition comes fast, you'll still have time to learn the various procedures you need to know. Depending on the position, you'll usually be given aircraft-specific ground school instruction, as well as five flying hours, with the possibility of a check-ride prior to flying in day-to-day operations. Preparation for this should take place as early as possible, even before you start flying. For example, if you're working on the ramp prior to flying, try to go along on flights to get a sense of the procedures, and follow along on a map to get to know the area. Make sure all your licences and ratings are current and be ready to make the move up at any time. The last thing you want is to finally be given the chance to fly and not be ready for it.

Once you do get called to the flight-line, spend as much time as possible studying. During this time, don't worry about your social life. Instead, spend as much time as possible absorbing information. Things will get much easier as you get used to your plane and your duties, but until then, focus on becoming proficient.

Risk Management

As a pilot, your main job is risk management. You're being paid to decide when it's safe to fly and when it's not. A familiar quote states, "The hardest part of flying is knowing when to say no." That's even more the case when you're first starting out. If your first flying job is as a First Officer, one issue that you'll have to deal with is knowing when to speak up and contradict your Captain. If your first job finds you flying solo, on the other hand, you'll have to make judgments as to when to go flying and when to stay at home. The phrase "It's better to be on the ground wishing you were in the air than in the air wishing you were on the ground" is no doubt true, but if you stayed on the ground whenever you didn't feel like flying, or whenever the weather wasn't ideal, you probably wouldn't keep your job for very long.

So how do you decide when to go and when to stay? Unfortunately, many new pilots have lost their lives flying into deteriorating weather conditions, all because of a lack of experience. You'll have to find your own comfort levels. The best piece of advice I can give you is to talk to more experienced pilots. Indirectly ask them what they would do in any given situation. Find out what their limits are.

When I first started flying as a Captain, I chose to err on the side of caution. The company I flew for had a rule of a maximum 10 knots allowable cross-wind (winds coming from the side of the runway) for new pilots. I was supposed to do a cargo run and the cross-winds were at roughly 15 kts. I've landed in cross-winds that were much higher than that before, but I felt that if the company had this rule then I was not going to be the one to go against it. I felt pressure from the charter coordinator to take the trip, but I thought what if I do this trip and heaven forbid, something happens during the landing? The first thing that would be asked is why I chose to go when the cross-winds were above the limits for new pilots on that aircraft. You have to think like this for all situations. You're the pilot, and if something goes wrong, it will be you who takes the blame, even if you'd been pressured into flying in unsuitable conditions.

The Canadian Aviation Regulations set out the limitations and regulations for flying. While some regulations are more structured and followed than others, you really have to think of it in terms of a worst-case scenario. If something goes wrong during the flight, the first thing the accident investigators will look at will be your conduct. If you disobeyed any of the regulations, they'll find out. In fact, if you're lucky enough to survive an accident, you'll probably be fined, charged, or even sued if you were breaking any rules when the unfortunate event occurred. While you might have felt pressured by your company, they didn't put a gun to your head and make you fly.

As a brand new First Officer, you're also in a tricky situation if you get in a disagreement with a Captain. On one hand, you're part of the crew and your duty is to keep the aircraft safe. On the other hand, you may be flying with a pilot who has considerably more experience and knowledge than you. There may be occasions when, as a new pilot, you may disagree with the actions of your Captain. In most of these cases, when the safety of the aircraft is not in jeopardy and the Captain simply does something a different way than you would, it may be best to not say anything or merely wait until you are on the ground and ask for a clarification of the procedure. However, you must speak up in situations where the aircraft or its passengers could be at risk.

A good Captain will listen to you and use your input when making a decision. However, you'll undoubtedly have bad Captains (or good Captains having a bad day) where speaking up will result in them getting snarky with you. If it does happen to you as a new F/O, don't worry—it happens to almost everyone. One of the toughest parts of learning to fly as a co-pilot is getting used to flying with different Captains. You'll have to decide for yourself when it's worthwhile to speak up and when it's worthwhile to just let things pass. For me, it depended on my mood. Generally, if I didn't feel that the safety of the aircraft was compromised, I would just keep my mouth shut and do what the Captain said. However, if there was ever a real threat to the safety of the aircraft I would speak up. A couple of times it made for an uncomfortable atmosphere in the cockpit, but I was happy with my decision to speak up.

The Check Ride

Depending on the aircraft you're assigned to fly, you may have to do a check ride with a company check pilot or a Transport Canada Inspector. Some aircraft will require a Pilot Proficiency Check (PPC) or an Aircraft type rating, both of which involve a check ride. If your aircraft requires a type rating, you will be required to have 250 hours TT and have written the IATRA (Individual Aircraft Type Rating – Airplane) within the past 24 months. It is probably best to write the IATRA right after you've finished your commercial licence because the information will still be fresh. For some of the smaller aircraft, usually the ones in which you do not fly IFR as Captain or are just a co-pilot, you only require a Pilot Competency Check (PCC), and no check ride is needed after the required training by a pilot. Check rides are always a nerve-wracking experience, and it will likely be even more so during your first one. There are a couple things to keep in mind. To begin with, you've already done a number of flight tests in your career, and for the most part, check rides follow the same basic procedure. You need to show someone that you can fly the airplane safely and diligently. Secondly, most pilots have blown a check ride at some point. There's an old adage (there are a lot of those!) in aviation: "There are two types of pilots—ones who've failed a check ride, and ones who *will* fail a check ride." While this shouldn't be an excuse for you to go into the check ride unprepared, it should help calm the nerves a bit. If you fail this ride, it's really not the end of the world or your career.

In a small airline, it's often hard to schedule training. As a result, pilots are often given last-minute notice to do training flights or check rides; it's one of the reasons so many pilots go into check rides with no real preparation. During your first check ride, not only may you be in an unfamiliar plane, but you may also be in an unfamiliar area. Therefore, it's imperative to prepare ahead of time as much as possible. Everybody's situation will be unique, but there are numerous things that can be done to guarantee that you will be well prepared. The most basic thing you can do is stay on top of your IFR skills. Even if you haven't flown for a while, go over charts, checklists, and if possible, practice on a simulator. Microsoft Flight Sim is a great way to practice instrument approaches. You can even get different aircraft for the program. One of my colleagues downloaded the Cessna 441 Conquest II program onto his version of Flight Sim, and he was able to practice instrument approaches using the company S.O.P.s and proper speeds. When the time came for training and check rides, he was familiar with the different controls in the aircraft.

Like many other flight tests, don't be surprised if the examiner also tries to teach you something. Many of the examiners are former instructors and have significant industry experience from which you can learn. Examiners are not out to try and fail you. If you have a company check pilot performing the test, don't think that you'll get off any easier than if it were a Transport Canada Inspector. Although you'll benefit from the check pilot having a better understanding of the area and your company S.O.P.s, they'll likely put you through the paces as hard as an inspector.

Being a Good Employee

One of the most common complaints I've heard from Chief Pilots who hire-entry level pilots is that they don't treat flying as a job. I'm not sure if this is because of immaturity, or because they're used to flying in a flying club or college atmosphere. Regardless, it's important to remember that when you're working as a pilot, you're an employee of the airline. This position brings with it some responsibilities, and not just those associated with flying. You also have responsibilities as an employee.

Most of these suggestions are common sense, but a reminder would be worthwhile:

Always be on time: This is one of the most important traits as a pilot and an employee in general. Flying is not a job where you can show up late on a regular basis. At the former Canadian Airlines, if you were late for just one flight, you would have a meeting with one of the Chief Pilots and the meeting would start with him asking, "Why should I not fire you?" Although it may seem extreme, it wasn't too far out there. You CAN'T be late for a flight. While there will no doubt be extenuating circumstances on rare occasions, it's critical to never be late. Make sure you take everything into account, and if you need to, give yourself extra time to make it to work. It's better to have some spare time before the flight leaves than to rush around at the last minute.

Keep a good attitude: Very often, how your day went at work will depend on your interaction with your co-workers. If you're stuck working with someone who's cranky, annoying, obnoxious, rude, or downright mean, it can make your day at work seem like torture. Don't be that person. In a sometimes highly stressful environment like an airline, there will no doubt be times when you'll get stressed out. Try as much as possible not to take it out on your co-workers. In fact, be patient, friendly, and helpful. This can be very tough, but if you get the reputation of always being a jerk, it'll end up hurting you in the long run.

Don't bad mouth co-workers: At some major airlines, you won't know the majority of your co-workers. In smaller airlines, you'll probably know almost everybody. In some respects, it can be like high school all over again. Do your best to steer clear of office politics and don't start bad mouthing co-workers. It's a good idea to form close friendships with a few of your colleagues. These are the people you can trust and talk to if something is bothering you. It's much better to vent your anger about a jerky co-worker to a trusted friend, rather than some random colleague.

Be humble: Too often, when pilots are first starting at a company, they can come across as know-it-alls. More often than not, it's unintentional. They just wish to be considered competent by their co-workers and have gone a little overboard. In general, pilots tend to be confident people, and they can come across as being very cocky. While self-confidence is an ideal trait in a pilot, being cocky to the point of aggravating your co-workers is not a good idea. Even if you know what the other employer or crewmember is telling you, don't come across as a know-it-all. In aviation, it's essential that every person is on the same page in any given situation. If you happen to know what someone's trying to teach you, don't be afraid to show them that you know it—just be polite about it. And if you're learning something new, listen and learn it! Even the most experienced pilots will learn something new from time to time—about the job, the company, the aircraft, or flying in general. You're a pilot, not God!

Don't try and do someone else's job: There's a fine line between being helpful and stepping on other people's toes. This isn't limited to aviation, but you'll need to be wary of over-stepping your bounds and trying to be too helpful. Perhaps you're trying to impress management (which in itself is not a bad idea), but if you do so at the expense of making a co-worker look bad, you won't be winning yourself any friends. Often, specifically in the case of dealing with dispatchers, you may be given a plan that, on the surface, doesn't seem to make much sense. Keep in mind that you might not be seeing the whole picture, and there may be a good reason why things are the way they are. Offering suggestions and finding out the information is always helpful, but sometimes you just need to do what you're told because that's your job.

Alcohol & Narcotics

The following section is vital, and all the information it contains should be remembered and practiced throughout your training and your future career as a pilot.

Flying requires absolute concentration. Nothing should be allowed to hinder your judgment, your cognizant ability, or your reflexes. Potential causes of a hindered ability to safely fly include being under the influence of any intoxicating substance or a lack of sleep. However, for the purposes of this chapter, we're going to concentrate on the negative effects of alcohol, prescription drugs, and illegal drugs.

One of my favourite quotes from the show "Family Guy" occurs when Brian and Stewie go on a cross-country adventure. They get hopelessly lost until they see a sign for an airport up ahead. "Hey look!" Brian exclaims. "It's an airport! And where there's an airport, there are planes. And where there are planes, there are pilots. And where there are pilots, there's a bar. I need a drink, let's go!" Obviously this is a joke, based on the stereotypical view that a disproportionate number of pilots are heavy drinkers. It's tough to tell if this "heavy drinkers" label is deserved, or if it's nothing more than an unjust stereotype. Either way, the idea is clearly contradictory when the stringent alcohol consumption laws for pilots are taken into consideration.

Canadian Aviation Regulation 602.03 states that no person shall act as a crewmember of an aircraft within eight hours of consuming alcohol, while under the influence of alcohol, or while taking any drug that impairs your faculties to the extent of endangering the aircraft or anybody on board. Many pilots refer to this regulation as the "Eight hours bottle to throttle" rule. However, two things should be noted. First, this rule is unique to Transport Canada , with the majority of other airlines requiring periods of twelve hours or more between drinking and flying. Second, you should note that Regulation 602.03 clearly states that not only is flying forbidden within eight hours of alcohol consumption, but that you also cannot be under the influence of *any* alcohol. If enough alcohol is consumed, eight hours is often not enough time for all traces of alcohol to have left your body. So you cannot, for example, binge drink all evening, go to bed at midnight, and then expect to go flying at 8 a.m. and not have alcohol in your system. Flying a plane is not driving a car. You might be okay to drive yourself home after a couple of beers, but as a pilot, the rule you must follow is zero-tolerance and nothing less. Before you fly, not a single drop of alcohol should have passed your lips in the previous eight hours (preferably longer) or you risk losing both your job and your licence.

So, what happens if you've had a drink and your company calls you and asks you to fly? Simple; you say no. You'll probably have to explain why you were drinking while you were supposed to be on call, but that embarrassment will have to dealt with and overcome. There can never be an excuse for flying after you've been drinking. A few times in my career, I've seen a pilot miscalculate their schedule. They mistakenly believed they were not on call, had a drink and then got called to do a flight. This happened within 8 hours of them consuming alcohol so they had to decline the flight and explain why. In most cases, these pilots got into trouble for drinking while on call. But that trouble was nothing compared to the trouble they'd have faced had they flown while intoxicated..

In fact, there was once a pair of pilots in the US that were caught attempting to fly while intoxicated. They were sentenced to a substantial jail term! I cannot repeat it enough—this is not something you want to risk. Set up a system for yourself that works. Know your company's limits and your own alcohol limits, and never break them. For me, I would not have a drink the day before I had a flight. Some pilots often go further than that, while some take the company's twelve hour rule for all it's worth.

This is what section 3.11 of the Airman's Information Manual (AIM) has to say:

> Never fly while under the influence of alcohol or drugs. It is best to allow at least 24 hours between the last drink and takeoff time, and at least 48 hours after excessive drinking. Alcohol is selectively concentrated by the body into certain areas and remains in the fluid of the inner ear even after all traces of alcohol in the blood have disappeared. This accounts for the difficulty in balance that is experienced in a hangover. Even small amounts of alcohol (0.05%) have been shown in simulators to reduce piloting skills. The effect of alcohol and hypoxia is additive and at 6 000 feet ASL (1 829 m), the effect of one drink is equivalent to two drinks at sea level. The body metabolizes alcohol at a fixed rate and no amount of coffee, medication, or oxygen will alter this rate. ALCOHOL AND FLYING DO NOT MIX.

Source: *3.11 in the Airman's Information Manual (AIM)*

URL:http://www.tc.gc.ca/CivilAviation/publications/tp14371/AIR/3-1.htm#3-11, Civil Aviation. Reproduced with the permission of the Minister of Public Works and Government Services Canada, 2007.

Prescription and over-the-counter medication can also cause side effects that may affect the safety of a flight. If you're taking any daily prescription drugs, you should mention it to your Medical Examiner. The examiner can then look into the situation further and decide if you're eligible to fly. If any drugs are prescribed to you following your medical, be sure to inform your physician that you're a pilot, as this is required by law. Your physician can then review the side effect of the drugs and the effect it may have on your ability to fly, and make a determination on whether or not flying is safe while using the prescribed medication.

Over-the-counter medication can vary greatly. Your best bet for any situation is to talk to your Aviation Medical Examiner—he or she will know best. Medications whose side effects include drowsiness are usually not permitted (this applies to many cold and flu remedies and anti-nausea medications such as gravol). Allergy medicines, on the other hand, are normally permitted. Consult your physician on all over-the-counter drugs prior to their use.

Illegal drugs are a controversial issue among pilots. No pilot would claim that it's okay to be under the influence of an illegal drug while flying, but some believe that the use of illegal drugs is not a problem, as long as ample time has elapsed between drug use and flight time. Others believe that as a pilot, there's no room for any type of illegal drugs in your life. This is an interesting debate, and without sounding like an after-school special, you should be very wary of using illegal substances as a professional pilot. In my opinion, there are two categories of illegal drugs: pot, and everything else. I know people, some of them pilots, who'll smoke pot on occasion, and it doesn't appear to have an effect on their daily lives. In fact, it could even be argued that the side effects of pot are less detrimental to overall health than over-consumption of alcohol. That being said, there are two important things to keep in mind.

First, despite arguments from many people that pot is less harmful than alcohol, it's illegal—alcohol is not. Are you willing to risk smoking pot? If you do, you risk losing your licence, and depending on the offence, may even be prohibited from getting a passport or traveling abroad. That's pretty important when you're an airline pilot!

The second thing to keep in mind is that marijuana is illegal, and therefore considerably less research has been carried out on its effects when compared to prescription and over-the-counter drugs. As a result, there's a lot we don't know about it. THC, one of the active ingredients in cannabis, is absorbed by fat cells and can stay in your system for a long time after you've smoked it. There was a crash a number of years ago of a medevac aircraft, in which both pilots were killed. In the autopsy, it was found that the First Officer had noticeable levels of THC in his system. While it was not directly implicated as a cause of the accident, no one knows for sure if it have an effect on the flight's safety. What would the effect have been had the First Officer survived? Would it have made a difference in the investigation? There's no right answer, but you start getting into very murky legal waters. In my opinion, even if pot really is completely harmless and you use it in a responsible way, the consequences are far too serious to risk it.

For all the drugs under the "Everything Else" banner, there can be only one opinion: avoid them at all costs. An illegal drug habit cannot co-exist peacefully with a pilot's career. Most of the drugs have serious side effects, and even if they were legal, a regular user could not obtain a pilot's medical certificate. And don't forget that they're illegal. It's like upping the stakes—being caught with these drugs can bring about much greater repercussions than being caught with a small amount of pot. Many of these drugs are also highly addictive, and for this reason alone, a pilot should never even consider their use. A final thing to remember—larger airlines will carry out a drug test during each of their initial medical checks. If illegal drugs are detected in your system, you could lose your dream job forever.

Being a Good Pilot

There are a number of ways that one can be classified as a good pilot. My personal favourite is the saying, "A good pilot is one who has an equal number of successful take-offs and landings." But there really is much more to being a good pilot than simply getting the plane and passengers back on the ground in one piece.

Always keep learning: After you've been flying for a certain amount of time, you'll begin to become comfortable with your plane and your job. While a certain amount of comfort is good, getting too complacent can be dangerous. There's ALWAYS something to learn while flying. If you close your mind to learning new things after you've finished your flight training, you're a danger to everyone on your flight and to other planes in the sky.

Airplanes are complex machines. They have numerous systems and, despite the fact that a basic working knowledge is all that's required to pass most exams, it's a good idea to develop an intricate knowledge of each system. When you're training, you may not have much free time to devote to this kind of learning. Once you start flying professionally, though, you'll have the necessary time. Try to learn new things every day!

Experience is a vital concept in the flying profession. You'll learn something on every flight you make, and you'll encounter new things and new problems on a daily basis. Always think about your actions. Analyse your decisions, and ask yourself why you chose one option over another. Find out if other pilots treat situations in a different way, or have a different approach.

There are a number of situations in flying where things are done just as a matter of personal preference. This is understandable, since no two people are the same. However, I've encountered pilots who constantly think, "This is the way I've always done things and this is the way that I'll always do them." These pilots don't even consider the reasoning behind the decisions they make. One of the Captains I used to fly with would often question me about why I was doing things a certain way. I actually found it quite frustrating, as every time I'd touch a switch he'd pipe up, "Why are you doing that now? Why are you doing it that way?" I thought, "Geez buddy, give me a break!" However, in talking with him I realized that he doesn't care which way I do particular things—he just wanted to see that I was thinking about my actions and knew why I was doing things. I began to look at his questions less as an annoyance and more as an invitation to discuss different ways of performing various tasks thus improving safety and communication in the cockpit.

Keep up on your drills: Besides learning new things, it's also important to remain familiar with your emergency procedures. Some people claim that flying a plane is like riding a bike, in that you never forget how to do it. This is not the case with emergency drills, though. It's very rare to use emergency procedures on a regular basis. In fact, except in training, I can count the number of times on my fingers that I've had to use an emergency drill while in flight. Since they're not used that often, they can be easily forgotten. That's why it's imperative to keep up on them. Find a way that works for you to keep up-to-date. Maybe get a co-worker or a friend to quiz you on them on a regular basis, or just plan to go over them every couple of days. This is kind of like going to the gym though you're exercising your mind, not your muscles. Find a system that works for you and stick with it. At my old airline, they used to have a section on the checklist for reviewing emergency drills. Unfortunately, in too many cases, the Captain would skip the drill and proceed directly to the flight. Occasionally I'd ask the Captain to quiz me on an emergency procedure, especially if I had training or a ride coming up. In hindsight, I should have done this more often. On one occasion, during a four-and-a-half hour flight on a plane without a bathroom, the Captain got me to ask him questions on every single emergency drill in the book as a distraction from his overfull bladder!

Help out: Pilots can generally be quite busy when at the airport. There's usually flight-planning, weight and balance, getting the plane ready, and numerous other tasks that may pop up when you're already running late. When you get a free moment, it's very tempting to take a bit of a break and relax. While this is something that you should feel entitled to do, it's a good idea to sometimes use this free time to help out in other ways. At many smaller airlines, there are separate cargo handlers who are often "pilots in waiting." It's often not possible to help out the cargo workers at the larger airlines because of union regulations. At the smaller airlines, though, the cargo workers will greatly appreciate a helping hand to load the plane. When you work at an airline, especially a smaller one, you're part of a team. Be a team player.

Treat your plane as if it was your dream plane- Very few pilots start their careers on their dream plane. Your career will usually begin as a co-pilot on a small twin-engine plane, or as a Captain on a single-engine plane. Most pilots dream of flying the big airliners and are not that impressed with a small, single-engine Cessna 206. But treat that 206 (or whatever your first plane is) as that big airliner! Know it inside and out, treat it with respect, take care of it, love it, kiss it …. Ok, maybe not…. But treat it as if it's the most important job of your life. If you get in the habit of taking good care of all the aircraft you fly, your bosses will see this and trust you to take care of bigger and better aircraft.

Be as helpful to maintenance engineers as possible: Pilots and maintenance engineers have a strange working relationship—each needs the other in order to do their jobs. If there were no pilots to fly (or break) airplanes, then maintenance engineers would have nothing to fix. If there were no maintenance engineers to fix airplanes, then pilots wouldn't have anything to fly (or complain about). Because of this mutual dependence, there will always be some friction between the two. As the pilot, there are a number of things you can do to make the engineers' jobs easier and improve your working relationship with them.

To begin with, never think you're better than them. It does not take more intelligence to fly a plane than to fix one, and just because maintenance engineers get their hands dirtier than pilots do does not mean they're any less skilled. That's not to say you'll never meet a maintenance engineer with a chip on his shoulder. Like all co-workers with an attitude, they can be difficult to deal with. Just shrug it off and don't take it personally.

If you're working for a smaller airline, take some time to get to know the maintenance personnel. Either at work or outside of work, make it a point to try and get to know some of them on a first-name basis. Doing so will create a better working relationship. Find out how they work to resolve maintenance problems. What type of write-up do they want? What type of description do they need of the problem? Usually the more detailed the description, the easier it is for them to resolve. After you've encountered a maintenance issue, try to personally talk to a maintenance employee to explain the problem. Having a discussion about what the problem is will make it easier to diagnose than if there were simply a note saying: "Engine is making a strange noise."

Finally, if the problem persists, don't blame the engineer. It can be frustrating to hand over the plane with a problem, wait all night for maintenance to work on it, and then have the plane returned with the same problem. While it's always possible that someone dropped the ball the night before and didn't do their job properly, it's not something you should assume. Trying to figure out what's wrong with a plane is like detective work, and as a pilot, it's your job to give the maintenance engineer as many clues as possible to help uncover the problem.

Read Transportation Safety Board accident investigations: As a pilot, it's important that you learn from your mistakes, and it's also imperative that you learn from other people's mistakes. While it may seem a little morbid, I highly recommend reading aviation accident investigation reports. It can be unpleasant to read how other pilots have died, but it's precisely for this reason that you should read them. The Transportation Safety Board (TSB) in Canada, and The National Transportation Safety Board in the US, conduct a thorough investigation in all aircraft accidents.

Available at:
http://www.tsb.gc.ca/en/reports
http://www.ntsb.gov/aviation/aviation.htm

These reports examine all the causes of a particular accident. As you progress in your training, you'll learn about the concept of the links in an accident chain. This concept addresses the fact that there's usually not just one cause of an accident. Instead, accidents are usually caused by a number of factors that, when taken together, produce disastrous results. The purpose of an accident report is not to assign blame. Instead, they attempt to identify each link in the chain of the accident. This allows recommendations to be made to reduce the chance of a similar accident happening again. If new pilots can learn from these mistakes, perhaps they will be less likely to make them in the future, and some good will have come from the tragedies of the past.

Being a Good Co-Pilot

Being a co-pilot or a First Officer can be a tough job. During your career, you'll encounter many different Captains, and each of them will want things done differently. Each of them will have different interpretations of their role as Captain, and your role as Flight Officer. The relationship is finely balanced between a co-worker relationship and a teacher-student relationship. Some of the Captains I've flown with were very good at teaching the co-pilots new information while treating them as a fellow crewmember. Other pilots I've flown with have been exceptionally poor at this. A common adage describes a good co-pilot as one that will put the gear up, put the flaps up, and then shut up! I strongly disagree with this.

A co-pilot, no matter what their experience level, is another crewmember and should be treated as such. Of course, if they're a relatively inexperienced pilot, they'll have less to contribute than someone with significantly more flight hours. They should not, however, be discounted simply because of something beyond their control. In an entry-level job, the position of co-pilot is a learning position. A few of the Captains I've flown with felt that it was not their position to teach. Needless to say, these were the Captains that were not particularly well liked by the co-pilots. In my opinion, while it's not a Captain's job to instruct, it *is* a Captain's job to teach. Generally, Captains have more experience and aviation knowledge than First Officers, and therefore, the knowledge is generally going to move from the left seat (Captain's spot) to the right seat (F/O's spot). While it may not be a direct lesson plan, the First Officer is learning while the Captain is "teaching." I personally think that the industry, especially Transport Canada, has dropped the ball in implementing standards for entry-level First Officer positions in Canada. I think that some First Officer positions should be treated as apprentice positions with a better definition of the duties expected of both the Captain and the First Officer and the teaching role that the Captain plays in the development of a new co-pilot. Transport Canada should pay more attention to stressing the added safety factor of having a co-pilot, instead, they tend to make it rather difficult for co-pilots to validly log hours on some planes and make it detrimental for airlines to require a co-pilot on some planes.

Treat every flight as an opportunity to learn something new. In a cockpit with a good atmosphere, you should never be afraid to ask questions, and you should NEVER act as if you know it all. I would even suggest that if a Captain is telling you something you already know, either let them finish, or be very tactful in letting them know you're already up-to-speed. A good way to do it would be to mention that you've gone over that particular topic, but then ask a related question. Not only will you avoid having to listen to something you've already heard, but you'll also be demonstrating to the Captain that you're willing to learn new things. In a cockpit with good communication, the Captain will instil a sense of teamwork in the crew. The crew should feel as though every member of the team is working towards a communal goal of providing a safe flight for everyone, while improving the knowledge and experience of each member of the crew.

It can be a tricky situation as a new co-pilot if the Captain does something you disagree with. If the safety of the aircraft is not in jeopardy, it's often best to keep your mouth shut. In some instances, of course, it's imperative that you speak up. Generally, you're going to want to be very diplomatic about how you approach the subject. A question looking for confirmation or a simple, "Just thinking about what we're doing—would it work out better if we did X instead?" might be a good way to get the point across. Sometimes a direct statement with a well placed "We" is helpful—for example, "I think we miscalculated the fuel load and we're going to have to stop before we get to our destination."

There will always be Captains you dislike flying with. The best thing you can do is take it as a challenge to improve your flying skills. Contribute as best you can, be safe, and just enjoy the view.

Hangar Talk – Being a Good Pilot / Co-Pilot

Take any job that gives you logbook time, but keep trying to improve the type of logged time (heavier equipment, variety of flying, busier terminals, larger companies). Keep an open attitude towards learning, and get involved with safety and/or training within and outside of the company.

—Chris Knox, A340/A330 Captain – Air Canada

Don't think like a co-pilot. Learn from every one. Remember that every day is a school day. Show that you're ready to make decisions and take command, while always being mindful of that chain of command, and run it by the other crewmembers This is all that a good Captain does with his crew. It shouldn't matter who is right but what is right.

—*Marc Paille, Lear 35 – Skyservice Lifeguard*

Patience. Work hard and roll with the punches. Brownie points go further than just sitting back and doing only what you're asked to do. Keep the big picture in your mind. Think about what you'll do when and if you have the choice of types of aircraft to command.

—*Chris Prodaehl, King Air Captain – Fast Air*

Keep your nose clean, and soak up as much as you can from the senior pilots in the company. NETWORK!

—*Colin Reeson, Piaggio Avanti Captain – FlightExec*

When it comes to flying and operational decisions, if you're being pushed into a situation you feel is unsafe, then be prepared to say no. If it means losing your job over it, then it's probably not the type of organization you would want to be involved with anyway.

—*Mike McDonald, B1900 Captain – Skylink Express*

Show them that you are smart and can be valuable as a crewmember but NEVER THINK OR ACT as if you know it all! Because very soon, you will realize that you have a lot to learn about everything (including yourself).

—*Susan Mileva, RJ First Officer – Air Canada Jazz*

Applying to Other Jobs

There will come a time, maybe sooner than later, when you'll want to leave your current job and begin applying for new ones. Usually this isn't an issue, but sometimes Chief Pilots or owners can be funny about having someone apply for other jobs. One of the first things you should do when thinking about changing jobs is put yourself in your employer's shoes. What will they think of your desire to leave? Would they be upset if you left, or would they wish you the best in your new endeavour? When you start applying for other jobs, you'll have to decide if you want to let your current company know about it. At some point, I believe you'll have tell them you're thinking of leaving; it might not be the best idea to tell them you're sending out résumés until you've received interest from another company. Telling them you're interested in leaving before you've received any interest from another company tells your current employer that you don't really *want* to work for them, but you will if you don't get any offers from rival companies.

If you have been at your job for a while and you have a good working relationship with your boss and you're not in line for any promotions in the near future, it's generally not a bad idea to let your boss know that you have an interview for another position. This way the boss knows to maybe expect a reference call and can also think about options for filling in your spot if you leave. Be honest with both your current employer and your potential new employer about the situation. You need to balance impressing your potential new employer with not burning any bridges at your old employer. At the same time, your new employer will be looking at what type of employee you are and how you treat your current employer.

Finding your second flying job will most likely prove to be much easier than finding your first flying job. Now you have experience that employers require and you fly to different locations on a regular basis and can meet new people. Many pilots I've met who've been looking for their second or third job will often have a few copies of their résumé in their flight bag. This is to ensure that they're well-prepared if they run into a potential employer.

Each situation is different. It would not be possible to outline the best way to act in all situations when applying for a second job. The biggest factor is respect. For the most part, if you treat both your current employer and your prospective employers with respect, you'll end up doing alright. Do not become known as someone who hops from job to job the second something better comes along. Actually, it might be a wise idea not to move from any job that you've had for less than a year. This rule isn't completely inflexible, but employers generally want at least a twelve month commitment from a new employee. Most want more than a year and will often have a training bond for a year or possibly two. If you're applying for jobs while you still owe money on a training bond, you'll have to weigh your options carefully.

Leaving a Company

When the time comes to leave your company and move on to a new job, respect is also extremely important. Depending on the situation, your current employer may have a difficult time filling your position. Therefore, I recommend giving them as much notice as possible. In most jobs outside of aviation, two weeks is the general required notice. In aviation, however, that may not be enough time. To make things more complicated, new employers often require you to start immediately. You'll have to figure out what's best in your particular situation, depending on how far in advance your schedule goes. It can be tough to work out, but resourcefulness can assist you. I've known pilots who've completed their training with the new employer, returned to their original job and put in two more weeks of work, and then began work at the new job.

Most Chief Pilots recognize the difficulty in changing jobs and will appreciate any effort that you make to try to make the task of replacing you easier. Nonetheless, you will still sometimes get Chief Pilots who take your leaving personally and will give you a hard time about it. This is unfortunate. While some Chief Pilots have no doubt been burned by a pilot leaving without any notice, if they still give you this attitude after you've made best efforts to give early notice there's not much else you can do. In this book I've stressed that you don't want to burn any bridges when leaving a job; however, sometimes it's best if you just move on (with as much notice as possible of course).

CHAPTER EIGHT: THE NEXT STEP

Flying is hours and hours of boredom sprinkled with a few seconds of sheer terror.

—Pappy Boyington

I T'S difficult to delineate the next level of progression in aviation. For some pilots, it's as simple as working the ramp at a company, working their way through the ranks on a series of different aircraft, and then getting hired by an airline where they spend the rest of their career. Other pilots have to change jobs and employers every couple of years in order to get experience on larger aircraft. Some airlines have a wide variety of aircraft sizes and types, whereas others only offer a certain size or type. For this reason, the distinction between a charter company, a commuter airline, and a regional airline can be difficult.

Between the smaller charter companies and the larger regional and major airlines, you'll find a spectrum of minimum requirements, hiring practices, pay scales, and benefits. Some will have relatively informal practices where networking is extremely important, and others will have a set hiring process with numerous hoops for potential new pilots to jump through. Some of the medium-level operators offer employment packages that make them desirable to pilots seeking a permanent placement. Others, however, offer relatively poor working conditions that make them merely a stop on the career ladder while you gain experience and flight time. The next step after a first job can vary greatly with each pilot. This is another time when I'd highly recommend talking with experienced pilots to see how their career progressed. There generally tends to be two typical next steps for pilots: flying for a larger charter company, or flying for a commuter airline.

Larger Charter Companies

As I'll discuss in Chapter 10, many corporate operators (and airlines) will hire their pilots from large charter companies. These companies will often have a diverse fleet of executive turbo-prop and jet aircraft, and pilots will likely have good customer service experience with a diverse amount of flight experience. It's possible that you'll one day be flying a scheduled charter flight to a northern mining camp and the next day you'll be flying a last-minute charter to somewhere in the US. This can be an exciting and challenging type of flying with lots of different experiences. On one hand, this can make it difficult to get bored with your job. On the other hand, always flying to different places can make things much more challenging and can add a big unknown to your schedule. Flying by the seat of your pants everyday can get just as tiring as doing the same flight to the same airport everyday.

For the most part, being successful in a job at a large charter company requires you to follow the same principles you'll already have learned—ones that have so far made you a good pilot and a good employee. Customer service will be vital—perhaps even more so than at your first job. Customers are paying big bucks to charter an executive aircraft, and they expect top-notch service. Not only do you have to provide excellent service while interacting with the customers, you may also face a fair amount of pressure from the passengers to attempt a flight even if the conditions are poor. Most passengers don't have a thorough understanding of aviation law and weather requirements. They've spent a lot of money to get from point A to B and they expect you to get them there in time for their important meeting. It can be quite a challenge explaining to them that even despite the fact that they've paid a lot of money for a private flight, they're still not going to make it to their meeting. Before you tell them that they won't make it, you'll be required to make your best efforts to find other ways to get them to their destination. For example, maybe there's another airport that is a short drive away from their destination that you could fly them to.

From there they could take a taxi the rest of the way. As a pilot for a larger charter company, you often have to be the problem solver in complicated situations. While the same holds true for jobs at an airline type job, it is usually more of a 'go / no-go' type decision rather than finding alternatives to getting the passengers to their destination.

Commuter Airlines

Commuter airlines, sometimes called "tier 3" airlines, generally operate aircraft with nineteen seats or less. They'll usually fly scheduled flights between city pairs that don't have the traffic to support larger planes, or where it makes more sense to do a greater number of flights per day with smaller planes. There are two main types of commuter airlines—those that fly the flights under contract for Air Canada, and those that don't. Air Georgian in the east and Central Mountain Air (CMA) in the west operate Beech 1900Ds under a code-share agreement with Air Canada. In order for a passenger to book a flight on their airline, they'd actually do so via the Air Canada reservation system. For commuter airlines that are not affiliated with Air Canada, passengers will book tickets directly with each individual airline.

Like the larger charter companies, the hiring process and employment benefits will vary with each of the airlines. Central Mountain Air usually requires approximately 1000 hours for a new First Officer, whereas Air Georgian requires 2000 hours for a First Officer on their Beech 1900. The benefits at these airlines are good—you get airline passes on Air Canada, and therefore have the opportunity to travel while living in a major city. This can be a nice change if you've been living in a remote northern community for a few years. The downside to the commuter airlines is the pay—it's exceptionally low in the beginning. As of the writing of this book, First Officers at CMA start at $22,500 a year and top out at $33,000 a year. Captains start at $40,000 a year and top out at $62,000 after eight years with the company. While experience from this type of commuter airline is looked upon favourably by Air Canada, all the First Officers I know at CMA have had to take a second job in order to afford to live in either Vancouver or Calgary.

A Central Mountain Air B1900D
photo by Mike Stefanski

Some of the commuter airlines that are not affiliated with Air Canada will usually carve out a niche market and stick with it, but it can be difficult to classify them as commuter airlines. Usually, they'll have a certain amount of charter business, as well as some regional airline work.

Commuter airlines can offer a unique type of flying that a few people will make their career. The high-end salaries for Captains are usually quite respectable, despite the often extremely low pay for entry-level First Officers. For the most part, however, this type of airline is used by pilots to build up time and experience in order to be hired by either a regional airline or a major airline. Nonetheless, all the tips about being a good employee and a good pilot that were discussed in the previous chapter still apply. Even if the main purpose of a job is for you to gain experience, you're a professional, and to be successful you must act as such.

Regional Airlines

Regional airlines generally operate aircraft with anywhere from twenty to ninety seats on board, with the majority of their flights lasting between forty-five and ninety minutes. Like commuter airlines, some of the regional airlines will have a mix of planes, which could include regional airliners such as a Dash-8, Saab 340, or Shorts 360. Air Canada Jazz is by far the largest regional airline in Canada. The other regional airlines are generally much smaller and focus on niche markets. Some examples would include Pacific Coastal and Hawk Air in British Columbia, Transwest in Saskatchewan, Calm Air in Manitoba, and Nunavut and newly created Porter Airlines in Toronto.

Flying for a regional airline can offer an airline-type atmosphere with good planes, a set schedule, and the ability to be home more than at a major airline. Requirements and salaries will vary for each airline, but generally, airlines want at least 1500-2000 hours with some turbine, IFR, and two-crew experience. Salaries for First Officers will usually start near $30,000, with Captains generally earning between $50,000 and $70,000.

Air Canada Jazz
http://www.flyjazz.ca/

Air Canada Jazz is Canada's largest regional airline. In fact, if measured by size of fleet alone, it's Canada's second largest airline. Jazz employs approximately 1450 pilots and operates a fleet of 135 aircraft, consisting of Canadair Regional Jets (RJs) and Bombardier Dash-8s. Jazz is a wholly owned subsidiary of Air Canada, and reservations are placed in the same place for both, although operations for each airline are quite separate. The pilots are hired through a different process, they have a different union, and their pay scale and benefits are different.

Prior to their merger, many different regional airlines would provide service to Air Canada and Canadian Airlines International. After the merger, however, Air Canada amalgamated these smaller regional airlines into one giant regional airline. The hiring process and administrative functions are now combined, and after a considerable amount of growing pains, the new company is now streamlined with much less overlap.

Air Canada Jazz CRJ
photo by Adam Van Dusen

Requirements

The Minimum requirements to apply to Jazz according to their job ad on Workopolis are:

Applicants Must:

-possess a Canadian Airline Transport Pilot's Licence (ATPL);
-have a minimum of 1,500 hours fixed-wing flight experience (only ½ of second officer time will be counted towards total flight experience);
-have a minimum of 1,000 hours pilot in command (PIC) experience;
-have a minimum of 500 hours multi-engine flight time;
-hold a valid Transport Canada Class 1 Instrument Rating;

-hold a valid Transport Canada Class 1 Medical;
-must be able to obtain an Airport Restricted Area Access Clearance
(i.e. security pass);
-hold a current passport and any additional visa documentation
required to operate aircraft within the USA;
-have completed a high school diploma;
-computer knowledge considered an asset;
-access to a personal computer with the ability to read Compact Disk
(CD) media;
-fluency in English; and
-be legally entitled to work in Canada

Pilot applicants far exceed the number of job vacancies available, so
preference will be given to candidates with qualifications exceeding
the basic requirements. Examples of such desirable qualifications
include, but are not limited to:

- experience in Airline Operations (i.e. CAR 705 operations);
- turbine engine experience;
- jet experience;
- heavy aircraft (i.e. greater than 12,500 lb. MTOW) experience;
- post secondary education; and
- French language ability

Job Details

Flying for Air Canada Jazz will provide pilots with a mix of
flying—a mix of what could be considered both airline flying and
regional flying. While the largest plane that Jazz flies is the 705 model
of the Canadair Regional Jet with seventy-five seats, most of the
planes that Jazz operates have between thirty-seven and fifty seats.
Flights could be as short as a quick hop between Vancouver and
Victoria, or as long as a four-hour trek from Calgary to Houston.
Most flights, though, will fall somewhere between one and two
hours. This could be a benefit if you prefer shorter flights with more
take-offs and landings, as I do myself. The downside to this is that it
will take a greater number of flights to fulfill your monthly hour
requirement.

Air Canada Jazz pilots are based in one of five cities: Vancouver, Calgary, Toronto, Montreal, or Halifax. Commuting may be possible, but the daily nature of the schedule would make it difficult when compared to the major airlines. As with Air Canada, Toronto is Jazz's largest base. New hires will generally be assigned based on need. There is, however, an opportunity to bid on different bases as seniority increases. A downside to this is that if the airline is ever forced to lay off employees, pilots may face the choice of either moving to a new base, or being laid off. This problem isn't strictly limited to Jazz, though.

Pay

Currently, new pilots at Jazz start at an annual salary of $35,000 for the first year and $41,000 for the second year. After the second year, pay switches to formula pay. First Officers will make approximately $50,000–$65,000, while Captains earn between $75,000 and $110,000, depending on their number of years with the company. Unlike Air Canada, where the pay is determined by the type of aircraft flown, a Jazz pilot's pay is determined by how many years they have been with the company. Therefore, a First Officer with four years of experience will make the same amount flying a Dash-8 as they would flying an RJ. This is beneficial, since pilots don't feel pressured to move up to bigger aircraft to make more money.

The Hiring Process

To apply to Air Canada Jazz, applicants must create an account on Workopolis.com and apply online. The interview is a four-step process consisting of an initial telephone call to confirm interest, an interview at one of Jazz's pilot bases, a medical exam, and then a flight simulator evaluation.

Interviews will usually take place at the Jazz pilot base that is closest to you. Jazz applicants are required to pay for their own travel to and from the first interview, although this is not the case for Air Canada interviews. Provided the interview goes well, Jazz will pay for transportation to and from the simulator evaluation. The initial interview is in front of a mix of pilots and Human Resources personnel, and consists of experiential and behavioural-type questions. The questions will be discussed in more depth in the next chapter. For the most part, there are not any extremely technical questions.

Depending on your particular situation, the medical may be done at the same time as the first interview. If this is inconvenient, it's possible to have the medical exam scheduled for a later date in a different location. I personally think that medical exams should be done *while* being interviewed—there really is nothing quite like trying to answer a few in-depth questions while having blood taken (kidding!).

The sim ride is done in either the DC-10 sim in Vancouver, the Challenger 604 sim in Montreal, or the Dash-8 sim in Toronto. The sim ride is analysed by the hiring committee to gauge your IFR skills, your two-crew communication skills, and your ability to learn things quickly. Flying a simulated version of a plane you've never flown in real life can be an intimidating experience, especially when undertaken during the interview process. While you shouldn't approach this situation lightly, the examiners realize that you have likely not flown that type of aircraft before—they won't expect perfection from you in such unfamiliar territory. What they are looking for is your ability to work in a two-crew environment and your IFR flying skills. If you remain calm and treat the flight as all your other two crew IFR flights, you'll likely be in pretty good shape. It's important to remember, however, that the examiners are testing to see how quickly you're able to learn new material. If you're continually improving upon your skills during your short time in the sim, they'll be impressed.

A few services offer practice simulator sessions for pilots in Canada. It's a tough call determining if this investment is worthwhile or not. Practice simulators can be extremely expensive, but the practice they provide can be invaluable.

Pros/Cons

In the past few years, Air Canada Jazz has expanded and more and more pilots are seeing it as a potential place to spend a career. Although the pay is generally quite low for the first few years, it quickly becomes a decent salary. When job benefits are also taken into account, such as flight benefits to all of Air Canada's destinations and a pleasant schedule, to name but two—life at Air Canada Jazz does not look bad at all.

If your goal is to fly for a major airline, working for Air Canada Jazz can still be a good move. There are things that should be noted, though. Prior to the restructuring at Air Canada and Jazz, Air Canada hired a large percentage of its pilots from its regional airlines. Therefore, getting a job at the regional airlines would greatly increase one's chances of getting a job at Air Canada. This is no longer the case. Following Air Canada's restructuring, they realized that it made little sense to hire a pilot for the regional airline, spend lots of money training them, and then move them on to the mainline where more money must be spent *retraining* them. Now if you're hired by Jazz, you'll not be eligible to be hired by Air Canada for two years. While there are certainly worse places to work while waiting for Air Canada to call, it would be frustrating if you're unable to take the job you really want. It's entirely possible that two years after you've been hired by Jazz, mainline Air Canada is no longer hiring.

If you're content spending a few years flying at Jazz, you'll gain valuable experience that will be looked upon favourably by other airlines. And if Air Canada never comes calling, you've still got a great job. The most recent rumour is that Air Canada is only hiring thirty percent of the pilots it interviews—not great odds. I'd much rather be turned down by Air Canada and still have a job at Jazz with the great benefits than at another job that may not offer such good benefits.

The schedule at Jazz is generally good. Unfortunately, you do have less of an opportunity to fly long haul flights and get all your monthly flying done with just a few flights than at a major airline. However, Jazz pilots generally have an easier time picking pairings that will allow them to be home at night on a more regular basis compared to pilots at major airlines. The downside of this is that the overnights that you do have are generally at less interesting or less exotic places than at a mainline carrier.

Jazz can be a good career move, but it is not necessarily the best career move for everyone. I have known a number of pilots who have turned down a Jazz job offer. Their career goal is to fly for Air Canada and they decided that at the moment, they had a job that they enjoyed and that paid better than Jazz and it would make more sense to remain at their current spot. At the same time, a number of pilots I know that have gone to work for Jazz are glad they made the switch and although the starting salary is a little low, they're really enjoying themselves.

CHAPTER NINE: THE AIRLINES

Big ol' jet airliner
Don't carry me too far away
Oh, oh big ol' jet airliner
Cause it's here that I've got to stay

—Steve Miller, 'Jet Airliner'

FOR the majority of pilots, the ideal career goal is to become an airline pilot. When the public generally thinks of a pilot, the idea of an airline pilot is usually the first that comes to mind. A career with the airlines, at least in the past, gave pilots a good opportunity for a stable job with a good income and schedule. Although things have changed, airlines still offer a combination of good pay, good schedules, and good fringe benefits.

Unlike previous jobs in the industry, getting hired by airlines is a much more formal process. Most of the larger airlines have individual human resources departments that deal with the hiring process. While having internal references will always be a plus, it's generally less important for getting a job with an airline than at lower levels in the industry. At the airline level, having a good résumé and cover letter is important. However, most airlines will generally use the points system or some variation thereof in deciding who to interview. The points system is a complex secret formula that assigns a value to certain types of experience, education, types of hours, and skills. Generally, the higher the education, hours, and skills set, the better the score.

This outline is intended to give you a broad idea of the hiring process utilized at each airline. In it, I'll be outlining the different things you should be doing in your career to make yourself more competitive when applying for these positions. When you have enough hours to start applying for airlines, there are a number of airline-specific books and interview courses to help you prepare. Aviation World—http://www.aviationworld.net/—has numerous books on the airline interview process. Amazon.ca and Chapters.ca also have a number of interview-specific books. Pilot Career Centre —http://www.pilotcareercentre.com/—offers airline-specific interview preparation courses. These courses can cost as much as $200-$400, but in my opinion, it's money well spent. You've spent your entire career to get to this level—why wouldn't you invest a few hundred dollars to improve your odds of getting the job of your dreams?

One of the most important factors in an airline job is seniority. Schedules, positions, and days off are all based on "bids." Date-of-hire is the primary means by which a person can bid on a good schedule. You are guaranteed your choice of days off only if pilots with higher seniority have not already made a bid for them. When you begin flying at an airline, it's likely that you'll be working most holidays—your schedule will not be that great. However, as senior pilots retire and more junior pilots are taken on, your ability to choose your schedule will improve dramatically.

In the following sections, you'll notice that the interview process at major airlines consist largely of experience-based questions. Specifically with WestJet, almost all the interview questions are in the form of "Tell me a time when...." Therefore, while you're progressing through your career, you should be making notes of these times. For example, interviewers will be quite impressed if you're able to recall a time when you went beyond the call of duty to provide excellent customer service, or when you were able to use teamwork to resolve a problem. These types of questions can be tough. While most people will no doubt have times in their career when they provided great customer service or used teamwork, it may be difficult to recall these situations on demand and under a high-stress situation such as a job interview.

The interview for your potential dream job is not the time to be trying to recall occasions when you were a great pilot and employee. Neither is the week or two before your interview. That's why it's a good idea to invest in an interview prep-course and keep good notes throughout your career. Pilots are lucky in that they're required by law to keep track of their flying hours in a logbook. You can use this resource to note specific situations that you might want to recall at a later date. You'll want to be careful what you write in your logbook, since interviewers will read it. Don't put things in your book that you wouldn't want an interviewer to see. For example, putting "failed the ride!" or "flew under a bridge" in your logbook notes would be a very bad idea (flying under bridges is illegal, and I do not condone it). Instead, put little reminders in your book that will help you remember a particular story. Doing this is great for keeping track of answers for potential interview questions, and it'll also help you remember your best stories to share with friends and family.

Today's new technology of e-mail and websites can be a great opportunity for pilots to share their stories. My love of writing came from writing my flying stories and combining them into a mass email. I'd send these emails to my friends and family, and they could share my experiences of flying in the north. The situations you experience on the road to becoming a pilot are interesting and entertaining, and remembering them could later assist you in landing a job with an airline.

Read over the various interview questions in the appendix. As you go through them, ask yourself which situations during your career might make good stories to tell interviewers. Make a note of anything you feel is relevant. Who knows—one of the stories you tell could be the one that lands you that coveted job at Westjet or Air Canada!

An Air Canada A319
photo by Adam Van Dusen

Air Canada

http://www.aircanada.ca/

Air Canada is Canada's largest airline and the 14th largest airline in the world, employing 3,200 pilots and operating a fleet of just over 200 aircraft (not including the aircraft operated by their regional subsidiary Air Canada Jazz). Formed in 1937 as Trans Canada Airlines, the airline was originally a crown corporation that operated with support from the Canadian government. In 1989, however, Air Canada was privatized. In the late 1990s, Air Canada merged with its rival, Canadian Airlines International. While this gave Air Canada a near monopoly on international air travel from Canada, the integrating of the two airlines proved problematic after years of fierce competition.

Even today, there's still some discord as to how the pilot seniority lists were merged between Canadian and Air Canada. At an international level, the merger happened at exactly the wrong time. As Air Canada was working to merge the two airlines, the events of Sept 11th, 2001 caused a massive downturn in the airline industry. Slumping air travel figures caused Air Canada to operate under bankruptcy protection from 2003 until late 2004. During this restructuring, Air Canada had to furlough (lay off) a large number of pilots. With the aviation industry slowly recovering, Air Canada was able to restructure and emerge from bankruptcy protection and is once again operating as a profitable airline and has recalled all of their pilots.

Air Canada currently has the majority of the market share for both domestic and international flights in Canada. As of Dec 2006, Air Canada was hiring approximately forty new pilots a month. Indeed, for the moment, things are good at Canada's largest airline. When things are good at Air Canada, things are generally good throughout the industry. Air Canada employs more than thirty percent of all pilots in Canada, so when they're hiring, it's safe to assume the rest of the industry is hiring as well.

Requirements

Here are Air Canada's minimum application requirements, taken directly from their website:

- ✈ 1,000 hours of fixed-wing flying time
- ✈ Completion of schooling to the university entrance-level
- ✈ Ability to pass the Air Canada and Transport Canada medical and visual acuity requirements for a Category 1 medical certificate
- ✈ Canadian Commercial Pilot licence, current Instrument Rating, and Multi-Engine endorsement
- ✈ Canadian citizenship or landed immigrant status

Pilot applications far exceed job vacancies, so preference is given to candidates with qualifications beyond the basic requirements.

Examples of desirable additional qualifications include, but are not limited to:

- ✈ Canadian Airline Transport Pilot licence

✈ University degree or college diploma
✈ Aviation College diploma
✈ Military or commercial flight experience
✈ Jet and/or glass cockpit experience
✈ Additional language(s)

Although the minimum flight-time requirement is 1,000 hours, it's very unlikely that a pilot with only the minimum experience would be hired. Most pilots hired by Air Canada have somewhere between 2,000 and 5,000 hours, with either turbo-prop or jet Pilot In Command time.

Job Details

One of the benefits of flying for Air Canada is their diverse fleet. For part of your career, you'll be able to fly mostly domestic flights, and other times you'll be able to fly mostly international flights. An entry-level position at Air Canada will likely be as a First Officer on the new Embraer 175 and 190, or as a cruise relief pilot on a Boeing 767 or Airbus A330 and A340. Some new pilots will also be able bid on an A320 F/O spot. A cruise relief pilot is a third pilot that goes along on long flights to allow the Captain and First Officer to leave the cockpit and rest during the flight. Being a cruise relief pilot is a great way to see international operations. The downside is that you never get to complete take-offs or landings.

The next promotion could be quick if the airline is still hiring and a number of pilots are retiring. However, if the economy slows down, it could be a while before a new pilot is able to upgrade. Air Canada operates over 100 Airbus A320s and their derivative A319s and A321s. The next step will almost undoubtedly be as a First Officer on the A320 family. After being on the A320 for a number of years, pilots will often have enough seniority to bid on a First Officer spot on a larger aircraft such as the 767, or as a Captain on the smaller Embraer 175 and 190.

Air Canada pilots are based in Toronto, Montreal, Vancouver, or Winnipeg. The majority of the pilots are based in Toronto. Where you're based can affect which aircraft you're able to bid on with your seniority level. For the first few years, during your time of low seniority, you may or may not have a choice on bases depending on what positions are available. It's often possible to commute to your base from other major cities served by Air Canada. Unfortunately, this may not be possible at the beginning of your career, since you are required to be on call more often than not. Being on call requires you to be located within close range of the airport at all times.

The schedule for airline pilots can be quite good. Most pilots fly an average of eighty to eighty-five hours each month. Depending on the length of your flights this could mean that you actually work as little as 10 days a month, however, it will usually work out to more than that.. Depending on a pilot's seniority, they get a certain number of GDOs (guaranteed days off) every month. At the lower level, pilots will get about ten to fourteen days off each month, but once a pilot gains more seniority and flies long-haul flights, this increases. For example, flying from Toronto to Hong Kong a few times every month would fulfill your monthly hour requirement, but if you flew the shorter flight, you'd have to fly between Toronto and Montreal many times to reach your hourly requirement.

Pay

At Air Canada, the starting salary is currently $37,000 per year— this does not include per diems. After two years, depending on the aircraft that they are flying, Air Canada pilots work on formula pay, which is calculated based on a complex formula of hours flown per month, type of aircraft flown, length of time flying, time of day flying, and time flown away from base. As a result, it's impossible to say exactly what the yearly pay for an Air Canada pilot is. However, not counting per diems (which can be quite substantial) First Officer pay starts at $50,400 on the Embraer, and tops out at $127,000 per year on the Boeing 777. Captain's pay starts at $96,000 and increases to $190,000 based on the minimum number of hours flown. However, with per diems and other added bonuses such as overtime pay, most senior Captains at Air Canada earn over $200,000 a year.

The Hiring Process

Air Canada has an online application process. Information can be found online at:

http://www.aircanada.com/en/about/career/pilots.html

The application process includes filling out an application form online as well as submitting a résumé. Be sure to update your profile every six months, or sooner if there has been a change in your employment status.

Air Canada will first call potential candidates to see if they're still interested in going through the selection process. If they are, they'll be invited to Toronto, Vancouver, or Montreal for two days of testing and interviews. Air Canada provides the flight for the interview. There are three steps to the interview. The first is the actual interview, the second consists of cognitive and psychological tests, and the third is a medical exam. The process of the medical exam has recently changed—it used to be done on the same day as the interview. Now, however, the medical is delayed until after the interview. Only after you've been offered a job is the medical carried out. If you pass the medical exam, the job is yours.

The Air Canada interview is done by two Captains on the hiring committee and one person from the human resources department. It generally lasts about one and a half hours and consists of general experiential questions. See Appendix 2 for a list of sample Air Canada questions. There are no technical-based questions.

The next step is the cognitive and psychological tests. There are three separate psychological tests with numerous questions. One is a 500-question true or false test. The other two tests each contain 100-150 questions, and those questions are of the never/rarely/sometimes/often variety. It's difficult to study for cognitive tests; I'd suggest that you just answer all questions honestly.

It will usually be at least a month or two before you hear from Air Canada. Successful candidates will normally be notified by phone; unsuccessful candidates will normally receive a rejection letter that invites them to apply again in six months. Successful candidates will be given an offer of employment that's conditional upon successful completion of the medical exam.

Pros/Cons

Flying for Air Canada is the career goal for most Canadian pilots. On average, Air Canada offers the highest pay for pilots, the best benefits, the most security, and the greatest opportunity to see the world.

Although the pay has decreased since their bankruptcy, Air Canada's pay structure remains the highest for pilots in Canada. While there may be a few choice corporate jobs that pay higher, in general, it is difficult to beat Air Canada's pay. The first few years are not that lucrative. In fact, most pilots take a pay cut when they start flying for Air Canada. In the long run, though, Air Canada's where the money's at.

Air Canada also has the most diverse fleet of aircraft in an airline setting in Canada. Most other airlines only have up to three different types of aircraft. Therefore, you might be flying the same type of aircraft to the same destinations for your entire career. Some pilots may enjoy this familiarity, but I believe most pilots would prefer a change of scenery once in a while.

There are, however, some downsides to flying for Air Canada. To begin with, the corporate culture is still quite fragile. After the merger with Canadian Airlines International and the subsequent bankruptcy and restructuring, current Air Canada employees have gone through a lot of stress. There are a number of employees who are not happy to be there. They're merely putting their time in so they can retire and get their pension. On a day-to-day basis, dealing with this type of person could be difficult. While this type of person is no doubt in the minority, it can still have a negative effect on you as a pilot. Luckily, many disgruntled employees took early retirement after Air Canada's restructuring—so things are slowly improving.

Jobs at Air Canada are possibly the most secure in the industry, although the security is not as high as it once was. The recent bankruptcy showed people that even Air Canada may be susceptible to the downturn in the industry. If there's another terrorist attack, or the price of fuel continues to rise, who knows how stable a job it will be? There were many pilots who were hired in the late 1990s who were laid off after 2001. Most of these pilots had to find non-aviation jobs. They were lulled into a false sense of security at Air Canada, and believed their jobs were secure for life. This led to them buying a house, a car, and fancy new toys—then suddenly their jobs were gone. The bills still needed to be paid, and so they were forced to find work wherever they could.

WestJet
http://www.westjet.ca/

A WestJet 737
Photo by Mike Stefanski

WestJet is now the largest airline in Canada after Air Canada and Air Canada Jazz, employing approximately 700 pilots. Founded in 1996, WestJet started up with a low-cost model of friendly, economical "no frills" service. Originally serving Western Canada with older model Boeing 737s, their friendly service caught on and they expanded into Eastern Canada. WestJet was successful during a time when the vast majority of North American airlines were laying off employees and losing money. Now WestJet has a fleet of 62 Next

Generation Boeing 737s. Although they still follow a low-cost business plan, they now offer in-flight TV service and have leather seats in a single-class layout. WestJet prides itself on its friendly attitude and good service. As a result, WestJet looks for potential employees who are exceptionally friendly and who have strong customer service skills.

Unlike Air Canada, WestJet pilots don't have a union. A lack of a union could be considered a good thing or a bad thing, depending on your point of view. Those against the lack of a union say that it could lead to WestJet taking advantage of their employees. WestJet pays less and offers fewer benefits than Air Canada, and some people believe a union would promote an improved pay and benefits structure. However, others argue that WestJet's lack of a union is responsible for their famous "positive work atmosphere." While WestJet employees are often not paid as much as Air Canada employees, in general, they seem happier and still make a decent salary. What's more important to you: money or happiness? Are they mutually exclusive?

Requirements

As per WestJet's website, the minimum requirements for applying are:

- ✈ Transport Canada Airline Transport Pilot's Licence (Aeroplane)
- ✈ 2,500 hours total time (Please note that if you have Second Officer time, only half of the Second Officer hours will be applied to total time)
- ✈ 1,000 hours fixed wing Pilot In Command experience
- ✈ 500 hours fixed wing multi-engine experience
- ✈ Valid Transport Canada Class 1 instrument rating
- ✈ Valid Transport Canada Class 1 medical
- ✈ High school diploma
- ✈ Legally entitled to work in Canada
- ✈ Hold a current valid Canadian passport. If you are not a holder of a Canadian passport, you require a Canadian Permanent Resident Card and any individual Visas necessary to enable you to perform the duties of a Pilot wherever

WestJet operates on a scheduled and charter basis. These locations are subject to change from time to time, but currently include the countries of Canada, United States of America ("US"), Bahamas, Cuba, Mexico, Panama, Dominican Republic, Jamaica, Netherlands Antilles and Honduras

✈ Possess valid Transport Canada Restricted Area Pass or be able to obtain same within 6 weeks of commencing ground school training

However, like Air Canada, most of the recently hired pilots far exceed the minimum requirements. Usually they have upwards of 4000 hours before being hired. Depending on how strong the industry remains, this may decrease. However, if there is another downturn in the economy you can look at minimums for airlines to increase.

Job Details

WestJet only operates one type of aircraft—the Boeing 737. Pilots hired will start as a First Officer and will move up to Captain as seniority permits, providing their performance has been satisfactory. Unlike Air Canada, WestJet's staff of pilots is younger, and the retirement rate is far slower.

Currently, Calgary is WestJet's only pilot base. There are some pilots that commute from other Western Canadian cities, but that can get tricky since WestJet generally has a lower frequency of flights than Air Canada. While there's been some talk of creating a pilot base in Eastern Canada, at the time of writing, there were no definitive plans to implement one.

Pay

Pilot pay at WestJet is a lot less complex than at Air Canada. Annual salary for a First Officer starts at $40,000 and tops out at $85,000. A Captain's salary starts at $105,000 and tops out at $153,000. One of the perks of working at WestJet is the employee stock option plan. Employees are able to set aside a certain percentage of their wages to purchase shares in the company, and the company will match the percentage they have invested. If the stock price remains the same, you've essentially doubled the money you've invested. If it goes up, then investing part of your income may be a very lucrative endeavour. There's still always the potential that the stock will fall, and you could potentially lose money. In the past decade, WestJet's shares have been a solid investment. This is still a gamble, however, without guarantees.

The Hiring Process

Prior to March 2006, the main focus of pilot hiring at WestJet was based on internal references. It was primarily about who you knew. In fact, for a while it was required that not only did you have to know a current WestJet pilot, you had to have flown with one in a previous job. As WestJet expanded, they decided to change their hiring procedures. Although a reference is helpful, WestJet now conducts their hiring on the points system, similar to Air Canada. WestJet's application procedure used to require applicants to apply via their website. Now, however, applications can be made through Workopolis.

One of WestJet's marketing tools is their company attitude. Their initial business plan was to follow Southwest Airlines' low-cost carrier model. Early on, WestJet didn't have TV's or entertainment systems on board their aircraft. Instead, for in-flight entertainment, the flight attendants and pilots would often tell jokes to keep the passengers entertained. While things have changed in recent years with an upgrade in aircraft and Live TV entertainment systems, WestJet still wants to hire people with the right attitude. As a result, this is one of the main criteria that they're looking for in potential employees. While flight experience and education are no doubt important, having the right fit for the company is one of the most important factors.

There are a number of different stages to WestJet's hiring process. To begin with, all candidates that WestJet is interested in will be contacted by phone. This phone call is simply to confirm interest. If the candidate confirms his interest, a phone interview will be arranged for sometime the following week.

The phone interview is performed with a Human Resources employee and lasts about forty-five minutes. The first half of the interview involves basic questions confirming that you have an ATPL and that your medical is valid. After the basics, they review your résumé and go through each item to make sure that you're representing yourself properly. They'll then ask you to elaborate on the types of duties, responsibilities, and career progressions you've had at other jobs. The last twenty minutes are spent discussing the terms of employment such as pay scales, uniforms, schedules, and the probation policy. Afterwards, provided there weren't any glitches in the conversation, the representative will suggest a date for a face to face interview.

When you first show up for the face-to-face interview, you'll be greeted by "Colleen the front desk lady." According to a few recent hires, Colleen acts as the gatekeeper. She's been at WestJet since day one and has seen almost every pilot candidate who's interviewed for a job. The common belief is that the hiring committee will often ask her opinion about potential candidates. While this hasn't been confirmed, by this point in your career it should be common sense that you treat everybody involved with utmost respect and friendliness. Before starting the interview, you need to check-in and get a visitor's pass, so make sure you get to the interview location at least fifteen minutes early.

After you've signed in, you'll have a written technical exam. This exam consists of fifty multiple-choice questions, and is based on the information contained within the Airman's Information Manual (AIM) and the Canadian Air Pilot—General (CAP GEN). While it's not overly difficult if you're familiar with each of these books, it definitely couldn't hurt to review these books beforehand. At the end of the technical exam, you'll be asked to write a two-page essay on one of four topics, usually relating to a technical aviation subject.

Pros/Cons

WestJet's growth has been phenomenal. Throughout the past decade, they've steadily grown and expanded their service, while still remaining profitable. Very few airlines have managed such a feat. The million-dollar question is—how long will it last? All industry experts agree that WestJet has a solid business plan, but is it stable enough to remain competitive? Although they began by offering low fares and a no frills service, WestJet's fares are now competitive with Air Canada's economy fares. Will they be able to compete successfully with Air Canada without running up the debt like so many airlines before them? So far, at least, things at WestJet are looking pretty good. Despite some growing pains, they've managed to revise their business model and still remain competitive.

As mentioned earlier, WestJet doesn't have a union. For the most part, this has not been a detriment to the pilots, since the pilots have a good working relationship with the company. Despite receiving less benefits and lower pay, in general, WestJet employees seem happier and more energetic than Air Canada employees. That being said, the WestJet atmosphere is not for everyone. A running joke among current and former WestJet employees is that the initial training is more about drinking the "company kool-aid" and falling in love with the company than it is about training for the actual job. They want you to not only be good at what you do, but to enjoy what you do. In my opinion, while it could be argued that WestJet sometimes goes overboard with their friendly attitude, I'd rather work in an environment where my co-workers enjoyed coming to work on a regular basis than in one where no one wanted to be there.

Other Airlines

While WestJet and Air Canada do the vast majority of scheduled airline flying and even a fair number of charter flights, they're by no means the only airlines in Canada. The other airlines are generally divided into groups labelled as scheduled airlines and strictly charter airlines. As mentioned in the first chapter, scheduled flights are those that an airline schedules at a particular time and then sells tickets for that flight. A charter flight is the renting of a plane to a travel company, normally for a group of people traveling to a vacation spot. In charter flights, the travel company will sell the tickets—not the airline. The situation is slightly more confusing in some instances, when some scheduled flights allow tickets to be reserved for charter passengers.

Compared to Westjet or Air Canada, charter airlines tend to pay their pilots a little less money. The pilots schedule is comparable with

Air Canada and WestJet. However, charter pilots can expect to work more weekends than pilots at scheduled airlines because of the nature of charter travel. The benefits are generally less impressive than at a major airline, but charter airlines still offer an attractive benefits package. Depending on the airline, it's also possible to get discount rates on vacation packages from time to time.

Skyservice
http://www.skyserviceairlines.com/

SkyService is a diverse aviation company with three separate divisions: air ambulance, business aviation, and the airline. The airline generally operates charter flights for various travel companies such as Conquest and Sunquest. Skyservice Airlines started operations in the early 1990s and now has a fleet of Airbus A319 and A320s, Boeing 757s, and Airbus A330s.

One of the interesting aspects of Skyservice's airline operations is that during the slow times in the summer, when less Canadian travelers are flying south, Skyservice will send a number of its planes and crews to England. Once there, the planes will fly for a tour operator during the busier European tourist season. This could make for a very interesting piloting career. You'd have the opportunity to live in Canada for part of the year, and in Europe for the other. The majority of the crew choose to stay in Canada throughout the year, though.

To apply to Skyservice, send a résumé to the e-mail address listed in the careers section of their website. There are no posted minimums for hiring, but depending on the state of the industry, 3,000 hours TT with experience on either larger turbo-prop or jet aircraft would be the experience level that's typically hired.

Air Transat
http://www.airtransat.com/

An Air Transat A310 decorated for Christmas
Photo by James Ball

Air Transat is a Montreal-based airline that is owned by a travel company. Air Transat operates a fleet of fourteen wide-body Airbus A310s and Airbus A330s. Air Transat generally focuses on flights between Canada and sunshine destinations in the winter, and Canada and Europe in the summer.

Minimums for Air Transat are 4000 TT with a minimum of 500 hours jet experience, or 1,000 hours turbo-prop experience. Although not mandatory, being bilingual greatly increases a pilot's hiring prospects.

Zoom Airlines
http://www.flyzoom.com/

Zoom airlines is an Ontario-based airline that operates four Boeing 767s and one Boeing 757 on scheduled Trans-Atlantic flights between Canada and European destinations in the UK and France. Zoom doesn't tend to hire many pilots since they operate a relatively small fleet of aircraft. When pilot positions are available, though, they're applied for via the careers section on their website. General minimum requirements would be 4,000-5,000 hours with jet experience.

SunWing
http://www.sunwing.ca/

SunWing is a new charter airline owned by SunWing vacations that operates three Boeing 737-800s. They offer mostly charter flights between Toronto and sunshine destinations, and a small number of scheduled flights between Canadian cities.

CanJet
http://www.canjet.ca/

CanJet is a Halifax based airline that at the time of writing is undergoing some major changes. Initially a scheduled airline serving Eastern Canada, in September of 2006, CanJet ceased operations as a scheduled air carrier. They now fly strictly charter flights but are a significantly smaller operation than when they were a scheduled airline. Prior to their restructuring, CanJet's minimums were 5000 hours TT with some turbo-prop or jet experience, however, seeing as they have laid off a number of pilots and downsized their fleet, it is not likely that they will be hiring a significant amount of pilots anytime soon.

Northern Airlines

Three other airlines that operate scheduled flights within Canada are not well known to many southern Canadians. These airlines, Canadian North, Air North and First Air operate a mixed fleet of Boeing 737 jets as well as a few different types of turbo-props and jet aircraft. These airlines offer flights from various cities and towns throughout the Canadian Arctic to other northern towns and a few major Canadian cities. This type of airline offers a very different lifestyle than those that are based in southern portions of Canada.

Both First Air and Canadian North have pilot bases in some of the major Canadian cities such as Edmonton and Ottawa. Pilots will often fly a rotation, spending a few days at a time at one of the northern bases.

While the thought of working in Nunavut in February may not seem as appealing as flying to Cancun in the middle of winter, flying in the Arctic is an incredible experience. I've spent a limited amount of time flying "north of 60," and it truly was an amazing experience. Flying for an airline where you'd be able to live in a major Canadian city, but still be able to spend your days flying around the Arctic, would be an interesting adventure for many.

The hiring requirements for this type of operation can vary widely. Some of the airlines are strictly jets, and therefore require a high amount of previous flight time, whereas First Air has mostly turbo-prop aircraft with a few jets for the busier routes. First Air, therefore, has considerably lower time requirements for new-hire First Officers than many other airlines. A new pilot would generally be hired for a spot on a turbo-prop aircraft and then be able to work their way up to a jet position. Hiring requirements and general airline information can be found at each airline's website.

First Air – http://www.firstair.ca/
Canadian North – http://www.canadiannorth.ca/
Air North – http://www.flyairnorth.com/

CHAPTER TEN:
CORPORATE AVIATION

The facts are that flying satisfies deeply-rooted desires. For as long as time these desires have hungered vainly for fulfillment. The horse, and later the motorcar, have merely teased them. The upward sweep of the airplane signifies release.

—Bruce Gould, 'Sky Larking' (1929)

FOR many pilots, corporate flying is an alternative to a lifetime of flying for an airline. Corporate jobs in Canada can have huge variations in pay, working conditions, schedules, destinations, and types of aircraft flown. Many corporate positions can offer a better fit for different individuals than the airlines can.

Compared to the United States, where it seems that every small business has their own private jet, corporate aviation in Canada is relatively small. However, many medium to large companies have their own corporate aircraft. Some companies will use them as a corporate shuttle, transferring employees between two or more company offices; other companies will use them for travel to meet new customers; other companies will use them to fly the bosses to their vacation homes on a regular basis!

The average pay for a corporate pilot job in Canada can vary greatly depending on the company. An entry-level junior first officer flying a smaller jet or turboprop could expect to make around $40,000 a year. The high-end salary for a senior Captain flying a larger jet would likely be in the $150,000 to $170,000 range. With both jobs, however, there's usually a fair amount of non-flying duties that are expected of the pilot when they're not flying.

With such a wide variation of available positions, it's difficult to describe each one in general terms. Each company will have different hiring policies, employment expectations, and general working atomspheres. There are some basic generalizations that I'll attempt to touch upon.

Hiring

More so than any other area of aviation, business aviation jobs are all about who you know. Most corporate flight departments in Canada have only one or two planes. Therefore, unlike airline jobs where you are likely to fly with dozens of different pilots, many of whom you've never met—at corporate jobs, you'll fly with the same few pilots on every flight. You'll be spending a lot of time with them both in and out of the cockpit. You'll likely hang out with them at the hotel and you may even share an office with them. Unlike airline flying, you will likely have the same passengers on most of your flights, and these passengers will often be the heads of the company for whom you are flying. These passengers will also have a very large say as to the status of your job, so it's imperative that you impress them.

As you have probably gathered, corporate fit is extremely important for business aviation flying. Therefore, finding someone for a job will be a unique process for each company. Some companies may have a more formal interview process, whereas others will only take on people they know. Networking is the key.

If you think you'd like to have a career in corporate aviation, there are a number of things you can do to improve your chances, both on the skills side and on the networking side.

For networking, besides following some of the more general tips mentioned in Chapter 5, you'll want to get into a position where you meet corporate pilots on a regular basis. Earlier on in your career, before flying, working at an FBO that has a fair amount of corporate traffic is a good way to meet these pilots. Being polite and getting to know the pilots will not land you a job right away, but if you're able to keep in touch as you progress in your career, you'll be in a good position. A number of corporate pilots have mentioned to me how they made their first contacts while still fuelling planes and working towards their licences. A few years later, those contacts were responsible for getting them their dream job.

If you've already started flying, usually the first step to getting a corporate job is to get a job for a charter company that usually does executive charters. Often you will fly to the same FBOs and be able to meet corporate pilots. As well, some of your passengers may end up being with a company that later purchases their own private aircraft and need pilots. Many executive charter jobs are almost as difficult to get as private corporate jobs. However, most charter companies will have a larger fleet than a private corporate operator and as a result, there may be more opportunity to start on less complex aircraft and work your way up in the company. For example, there are a number of companies that operate smaller turbo-props like a Piper Cheyenne or Beech King Air as well as medium to large jets such as a Citation or Challenger.

The very minimum amount of hours required to be hired for an executive charter operator is usually in the 1,000 hours range. However, this is extremely variable. Although very rare, I've heard of people with less time getting a co-pilot spot. More often you're looking at anywhere between 1,500-2,500 hours for a medium-sized corporate charter company located in a larger urban centre.

For private corporate operators, a minimum of 2,500-3,000 hours, preferably either with time on type or jet time is desirable. This number will also vary depending on the size of aircraft the company uses. For example, if a company has a smaller twin-engine Turbo Prop such as a King Air or a smaller business jet such as a Citation Jet, they'll likely not require the same amount of experience as a company that operates a large Gulfstream IV. At the low end, operators of turbo-props and small jets may hire a co-pilot with roughly 1,500-2,000 hours. At the upper end, operators with the larger corporate jets will want a minimum of 5,000 hours with time on type.

A Beech King Air
Photo by James Ball

In this respect, you usually have to start on the smaller planes and work your way up. In some companies, where there are different types of aircraft in the fleet, you may be able to make this progression simply by remaining at the company. That being said, if you're in a stable position where the pay, job conditions, and benefits are all good, you may not want to fly larger aircraft. Although pay is usually related to the size of the business aircraft, bigger is not always better.

One of the downsides of business aviation is the relatively low amount of flying that most pilots do on a regular basis. A person's point-of-view will usually depend on where they are in the industry. Most corporate pilots fly less hours in a year when compared to pilots of charter companies or airlines. While this may prove beneficial for someone who wants to be home more, it can be difficult for someone who's looking to accumulate hours. This, however, raises two points. The first point: just because you fly fewer hours does not mean that you'll be home more often; business aviation often requires you to wait around for your passengers while they're in meetings or on vacation. The second point: it's not a good idea to move into corporate aviation with the sole intention of building hours. I've heard of some low-time pilots securing their 'dream' job through connections they've made, only to realize a year or two later that this type of flying is not what they expected it to be.

Although they're enjoying the position, with a low accumulation of hours and not much Pilot in Command time, they won't be moving into the left seat anytime soon. With this low accumulation of hours, it's difficult to gain a position in other parts of the industry. Essentially, they've become stuck in the right seat, although there are worse positions in which one can be stuck. Nevertheless, having your career progression stalled can be an extremely frustrating experience. As with any employment position, be sure to look at the long-term consequences before accepting any position. It may seem like a co-pilot spot on a business jet is a better option than flying cargo in the north, but in the long-run, you may be better off choosing a job that will allow you to fly more hours and offer more opportunity to fly as Captain. A couple of years later, it may then be the right time to move into a position where you are content being "stuck" in the right seat.

Pros/Cons

Although every job has its challenges, there are a number that are unique to Business Aviation. Depending on the company you work for, you may end up essentially being the private chauffeur for the owner or president. While every passenger and owner is different, one of the biggest complaints I've heard from corporate pilots is that they're at the beck and call of the aircraft's owner. Trips are often planned or cancelled at the last minute—sometimes this is due to cancelled meetings, meetings that last longer than expected, or the boss who simply chooses to stay and extra day or leave a day sooner. Unlike airline flying where you leave at a scheduled time, in business aviation, you'd likely lose your job if you left without your passengers! Passengers are often late and don't mind making you wait around, but they never want to have to wait for you! I was talking with some corporate pilots from the US one day, and they recalled a time when they were sitting in a hotel restaurant that overlooked the airport. They were leisurely eating their breakfast; their scheduled departure time still five hours away. They watched as a limo drove up to the plane and their passengers hopped out. Their meeting had finished early, but no one had told the pilots! In this case, the passengers weren't too upset, but they were annoyed they had to wait while the pilots got ready. Needless to say, the pilots didn't finish their breakfast.

An American registered GulfStream GV waiting for its passengers.
Photo by Adam Van Dusen

Corporate pilots also end up doing a lot of waiting around. This can be a mixed blessing. Sometimes the waiting around is at nice hotels in the Caribbean. Other times, you'll spend the whole day waiting around the airport or at a hotel in an industrial area near the airport. If you're the type of person who doesn't like a lot of downtime, this could be frustrating. Some corporate pilots utilize this downtime to focus on other income opportunities. Many FBOs have wireless internet access, and some corporate pilots who are internet savvy have used this time to their advantage.

Most jobs in the aviation industry have a certain degree of inherent instability, and corporate flying jobs are particularly unstable. When a company is going through a rough patch, the first cost-cutting measure is often to get rid of the flight department, or at least some of their aircraft fleet. This is entirely company-specific. Some company flight departments are quite established and are therefore just as stable as airlines, but there are others that do not last long at all. It can be difficult to figure out how stable a particular company's flight department is. Business moves quickly and you never know for sure what will happen to your company. One day you could be happily flying your bosses, and the next day the company has been bought out and the corporate flight department is slashed.

Despite this, most of the corporate pilots that I've talked to thoroughly enjoy their jobs. Some have worked at the airlines and found that they just didn't like the repetitive nature of the airline schedule. Others find they like having a working relationship with their passengers, and that they're able to talk to them on a first-name basis. Whether or not you'd enjoy a career in corporate aviation depends largely on the individual. I think it's wise, though, for all beginning pilots to look into the opportunities in business aviation. It's a good idea to talk with pilots who fly for a corporate flight department and investigate what they like and dislike about their job.

CHAPTER ELEVEN: OTHER FLYING CAREERS

More than anything else the sensation is one of perfect peace mingled with an excitement that strains every nerve to the utmost, if you can conceive of such a combination.

- Wilbur Wright

Most pilots' career goal is to one day secure a job with an airline or a corporate flight department. There are many other lucrative jobs in the aviation industry, though, and they should not be overlooked. The following is a list of some of those alternative job choices. Although this list is not exhaustive, it's a good start. Much more information on these, and many other potential jobs, will be available to you throughout your career.

Instructing

The vast majority of pilots who become instructors generally do so to build up their hours. There are, however, a number of instructors who genuinely love teaching people to fly and decide to make a career out of instructing. This is a good thing. At the lower levels, instructing is not lucrative, but a comfortable income is possible once enough experience is gained.

The typical aviation advice in regards to instructing is: unless you want to become a career instructor, the maximum amount of instructing time you want to achieve is 1,000 hours. While the validity of this statement can be argued, the point is clear: if you're instructing simply to build time, be careful not to accumulate too *much* time. However, if you want to stick with instructing, there are some unique opportunities.

As one progresses through the various levels of instructor ratings, the amount of pay increases. In fact, at a number of flight schools, positions of Chief Flight Instructor have salaried-base pay, plus extra pay for each flight you do. Therefore, you get the best of both worlds: a guaranteed salary, and the ability to earn some extra money by putting in more hours. After you've instructed for a while, becoming a Designated Flight Test Examiner is a good way to increase your experience. As you'll be acting for the government, the pay is generally quite good. At the same time, you still have the luxury of scheduling your flights when you want them.

Flight Colleges tend to pay better wages to flight instructors than regular flight schools. In fact, many of the colleges pay a decent salary that still affords you the opportunity to do some other instructing or flight-testing on the side. While an instructor won't get as many days off as an airline pilot, they'll be home almost every night and they get to choose when and where they work. Obviously, there has to be some leeway to accommodate students who are essentially your customers, but you generally have more latitude in the matter.

Bush Pilot

Similar to flight instructing, many pilots get their start flying either wheels or floats in the "bush." Most plan on going up north for a few years, getting their experience, and then moving back to the city. Flying in Canada's north is a challenging and unique adventure. Some pilots get up there, find they really love it, and are happy to keep doing it for the rest of their life. Flying to remote towns in "real" planes without lots of fancy autopilot and avionics equipment is the dream job for many. For people who enjoy spending time outdoors, it doesn't make sense to move to a major city.

A DHC-2 Beaver on amphibious floats
Photo by Adam Van Dusen

While most pilots will generally feel the push to fly bigger, more complex planes, there are a number of pilots who are content flying the smaller planes. I knew one pilot who had over 12,000 hours on little twin-engine Britton-Norman Islanders! He moved up to a 'bigger' single-engine Cessna Caravan for roughly the last 5,000 or so hours of his career. He loved his job and had no desire to fly for a major airline.

If a pilot is only interested in flying floats for the rest of his career, there are available options. The first is to stay in the north and fly seasonally on the larger floatplanes. An experienced float pilot can usually fetch a pretty decent salary, but the lack of work during 4-6 months of the year would hit the pocket book hard. This could be a good thing or a bad thing depending how you look at it. The time off could be beneficial to work on other projects. Another option for flying floats is look for work in some of the larger cities. Vancouver, for example, operates many floatplanes. They are usually sought-after jobs and therefore require a relatively high number of hours. Due the warmer climate, you're able to fly almost all year and live in a city. The pay will never be comparable with that of an airline or corporate operator, but there are a number of immeasurable benefits that may make it a great career for some.

Water Bomber Pilot

Flying a water bomber is an exciting variation of using an aircraft as a tool. There are three types of aircraft used as water bombers. The first type is the Canadair CL-215 and CL-415 water bombers, which are aircraft designed specifically for fighting fires. They have wheels, but have an amphibious fuselage that allows them to land on water or skim across it at high speeds to collect water. The second type of aircraft is an air tanker. These are former commercial aircraft that have been fitted with a large tank under the fuselage; a modification that allows them to hold massive amounts of water or fire retardant. Unlike the amphibious bombers that are able to refill their water tank at the nearest large lake, the tankers have to fill up on the ground at an airport before they can drop another load. The last type of aircraft used in water bombing is the small tanker. These are typically crop-duster aircraft that have been converted to carry large quantities of water or fire retardant. Like the larger air tankers, small tankers need to return to the nearest airport before they can refill their tank.

Most provinces operate some sort of Forest Fire Aerial Protection service, although the type of operation utilized by the province can vary greatly. Some provinces, such as Manitoba, operate their own fleet of fire suppression aircraft. Other provinces simply contract out the work each year to a company that operates forest fire management aircraft. Because of the disparity between provinces, there is no set hiring process.

For Provinces like Ontario and Manitoba that operate their own fleet of aircraft, you need to get on with the provincially owned air service. Most provinces operate a fleet of different aircraft not just for fire fighting, but also for executive transport for government VIPs and provincial employees who travel on a regular basis. In these type of flight departments, to get hired flying a water bomber, generally you're required to first obtain a position with the provincial air service and then after spending a few years there, bid on a water bomber position. Provincially owned air services usually require a fair amount of flight time, with a significant amount of float and multi-engine time.

CL-415s owned by the Quebec Government
Photo by Mike Stefanski

To fly for one of the forest management companies such as Conair, applicants are first hired to fly a "bird dog" aircraft. Only then will they move on to a job flying a tanker. Different companies have different minimums, but they'll usually be between 1,000 and 2,000 hours, with a fair amount of PIC and multi time.

Water bombing positions are quite popular. Not only do they offer an exciting form of flying that you can't get with a regular airline, they offer a competitive salary and a good schedule. Although during the summer forest fire season you could be working almost every day, most forest fire management operations pay their pilots a competitive year round salary so that pilots can have time off in the winter to either relax or work another job.

Geo-Surveying

Geo-surveying is another way in which an aircraft can be used as a tool. Geo-surveying includes a mix of aerial photography combined with other types of advanced scientific measuring equipment that is mounted on an airplane base to examine the ground that the plane is flying over. There is a breadth of functions that geo-surveying can be used for. Often these uses include mineral exploration and soil analysis.

Flying for a geo-surveying company can be a challenging job. While most pilots generally don't make a career out of geo-survey flying, there is the potential for a stable job. Pilots are paid well and most often work a rotation schedule: a few months on, one month off. Sometimes the flying is based in Canada near the pilot's place of residence, but more often, flying is done in the far-reaches of the globe. One month you could be flying over the jungles of South America, and the next you could be somewhere in the Arctic. The location can change dramatically. The type of flying that's done can also vary. Often, geo-surveying requires pilots to fly for long hours in specific patterns. This can be a challenge and can be tedious at times. Of the pilots that I've talked to who have spent time geo-surveying, some thought it was great, while others absolutely hated it.

Transport Canada Inspector

Transport Canada is the government's regulatory body responsible for regulating the aviation industry in Canada. As a result, Transport Canada needs employees who are experienced in the industry to help enforce the aviation regulations. Roles at Transport Canada can include conducting flight tests for various companies' pilots, doing random spot checks and safety inspections, and ensuring that individual airlines have the necessary emergency and training procedures in place. At Transport Canada, there is an opportunity to do a number of different jobs.

There are a number of downsides to working as an Inspector with Transport Canada. To begin with, there will be a lot of pilots who won't like you. While you might think that enforcing safety standards for all operators would be a good thing, there's a general perception within the pilot community that Transport Canada is not fair or reliable in enforcing these rules. I don't know enough inside information to be able to comment, but from my experience in the industry, it does seem as if Transport Canada too often works against operators and pilots. I think that, while enforcement is important, it sometimes seems that Transport Canada is more focused on threatening and scaring pilots with punishment than with working together with the other professionals in the industry to improve safety. Although I have met a few Inspectors that tend to reinforce this point of view, the vast majority of Transport Canada Inspectors I have dealt with have been extremely professional and fair.

Regardless, there is a need for Transport Canada Inspectors with experience in the industry. The pay is very good and, being a government job, the benefits and schedule are very good as well. One of the other downsides of this job is that you don't actually get to fly very often. While Transport Canada has a fleet of Cessna Citations, King Airs, and Twin Otters, Inspectors' duties primarily involve paperwork or other duties, whereas the flying is secondary.

Test Pilot

Canada is not home to many test pilots, although there is still a demand for them, particularly from aircraft manufacturers. Test pilots often play a key role in the development of new aircraft. Although computer design technology is very accurate in predicting the flight characteristics of a new aircraft, national certification bodies require a significant amount of flight-testing to ensure that each aircraft is safe for operation. To become a test pilot, one usually has to have a significant amount of flying time, an aerospace engineering background, and have attended a test pilot school. There are a handful of test pilot schools in the world, most of which are operated by various branches of a country's armed forces; these schools require pilots to be a member of the military forces to be eligible to join. There is a civilian test pilot school, The National Test Pilot School, in California. This school is strictly for civilian students. The Empire Test Pilot School in England is operated by the Royal Air Force. In certain circumstances, however, they permit civilians to join.

Test pilots will usually be employed by aircraft manufacturers or research institutes such as the National Research Council of Canada. Becoming a test pilot requires significant amounts of experience and education, as well as a fair bit of luck.

CHAPTER TWELVE: SO, DO YOU WANT TO BE A PILOT?

I live for that exhilarating moment when I'm in an airplane rushing down the runway and pull on the stick and feel lift under its wings. It's a magical feeling to climb toward the heavens, seeing objects and people on the ground grow smaller and more insignificant. You have left that world beneath you.

You are inside the sky.

—Astronaut Gordon 'Gordo' Cooper, 'Leap of Faith,' (2000)

I N this book, I've attempted to paint an accurate picture of some of the key things to think about when deciding if a career as a pilot is for you. There are many pros and cons. There are amazing benefits, but also hard challenges that one will face on the road to becoming a pilot. Besides the issues that I've discussed throughout this book, I think there are a number of key questions someone should ask themselves when deciding if they would like to be a pilot. There's no right answer, and no single question should decide your career path. These are just things to think about.

Why Do You Want To Be a Pilot?

This can be a tough question to answer. Even for current pilots, there's likely more than one answer. Some pilots say that one should only become a pilot for the love of flying and job satisfaction. That answer has always seemed ambiguous to me. Regardless, many of the pilots I've talked to honestly cannot fathom doing anything else. For them, nothing else would give them the same thrill as being a pilot.

There are many different reasons why people want to become a pilot. Below is a list of some the reasons that perhaps shouldn't be used as the only deciding factor in your decision to become a pilot. If one or more of these reasons are all that's inspiring you to become a pilot, you may want to rethink your career goals:

- money
- it's cool
- I watched Top Gun and wanted to be Tom Cruise
- it's easy
- it'll impress women
- I love living in hotels
- I want to see the world
- you get lots of time off
- it's glamorous
- I'll be flying for a big airline as soon as I get my licence

There may be some validity in each of these reasons (I mean, who *doesn't* want to be Maverick?), but if there aren't any other reasons that make you want to become a pilot, I can guarantee you that you'll one day regret your career path.

Do You Require a Set Schedule?

It's a nice feeling—knowing what time you start work, what time you finish, and what time you'll be home. Planning special events such as parties and birthdays are easier when you can easily judge when you'll be working and when you'll be off. For most careers, this isn't an issue. You work during the week, have weekends off, and you know what time you'll be going home every night. In aviation, this is the exception and not the rule. You'll not only work odd hours, but you'll also have uncertainty regarding your schedule. This can lead to much frustration.

At the lower levels of the industry, it's not uncommon to have very little advanced notice of your schedule. I've often heard of a company's dispatch calling up pilots in the morning and saying, "By the way, you have the day off today." This uncertainty tends to improve as you gain more experience, but even if you're with a large airline, you'll fail to have complete control over your schedule. This is especially true when you have low seniority, when you know that you'll be working almost every holiday. Often friends and loved ones just don't understand when you let them down because of last-minute changes to your schedule. Trying to buy tickets for a concert or sporting event is almost impossible.

There are still benefits to this lifestyle. Sometimes you'll get more downtime than a regular job, and as a result you can relax and work on various projects or other sources of income. Depending on the airline, you may also have flight travel benefits, so if you do have a week off, at least you can travel somewhere inexpensively. I'd been so used to traveling standby that it was a bit of a shock when I returned to school and no longer had flight passes and had to book my flights weeks in advance. I was used to being able to decide to go on a trip a day or two in advance. Now without the passes, I need to book things months in advance. Personally, I miss the passes.

How Do You Handle Being Away From Home?

Being a pilot can put a strain on family life. As mentioned above, it can be difficult to schedule special events, and you're often away for the holidays. On top of that, the job itself entails being away from home on a regular basis. I was talking with a former Canada 3000 pilot, and he mentioned that he loved his job even though he was away from home eighteen days in a row every month. Personally, I don't mind being away from home now and again, but being gone more than I was home would not be my idea of a great schedule.

Is this something that you can handle? If you've just started a family, or you're planning to in the near future, being away can be very challenging. A phone call can't replace a loved one's embrace.

Living in hotels gets very old very quickly. While it's great to be able to explore new cities and experience new things, often you just want to be home sleeping in your own bed. Pilots and Flight Attendants have a higher than average divorce-rate. The uncertain schedule and frequently being away from home leads to what is referred to as a.i.d.s. (aviation induced divorce syndrome). This is not to say that someone is doomed to be single for the rest of their life if they choose to be a pilot. I know many happy couples who have remained together throughout an aviation career. All marriages and relationships take work, commitment and effort, however, a relationship in which one or both of the partners is a pilot may require a little extra effort.

As with most lifestyles, there are advantages as well as disadvantages. If you have a supportive partner, a relationship where you get more space from each other can actually be quite fulfilling. Absence makes the heart grow fonder, as the saying goes. Being away from loved ones can help you better appreciate your time with them. When you *are* at home, you're often completely free for a few days in a row instead of being busy with work. So while the quantity of time you're at home may be less than you'd like, the quality of the time may be significantly improved.

There isn't a right answer. Almost every job requires a balance between work and social life. Being a pilot simply offers some complex circumstances that should be examined before starting out.

Do You Have The Intestinal Fortitude to Get the Job Done?

Being a pilot is often described as hours and hours of pure boredom punctuated by moments of shear terror. While I think this is obviously exaggerated, it does hold some truth. 98 percent of flying is routine and calm in nature, but there are always going to be downright scary moments. The bulk of training, especially after you've learned the basics of flying, is practicing emergency situations. Although it's very rare that you'll face an emergency, it's dealing with these emergencies where pilots truly earn their pay. Can you deal with that? How do you react under stress? Can you still focus when the adrenalin is pumping and there's a chance you could crash if you don't handle the situation appropriately?

Thankfully, emergencies are quite rare, but there are also a number of normal situations that require skill, practice, and the ability to remain calm under pressure. Landing a plane in bad weather with gusty winds and low ceilings, for example—now that's an intense experience! Are you the kind of person who'd relish that challenge, or would you rather not have to deal with something so tricky? Although you have to properly manage the risk and follow the law, diverting or cancelling a flight every time the weather isn't perfect will annoy your passengers *and* your employer

The unfortunate reality is that planes do sometimes crash, and people sometimes die. Flying is still the safest means of transportation, but there's always a danger that you'll go to work one day and never come back. I'd argue that this risk is actually less than the risk associated with commuting to and from work each day in heavy, rush-hour traffic. Having said that, the risks associated with flying should not be forgotten.

How Much Do You Value Your Sleep?

There are specific laws that dictate the amount of rest pilots must have between flights. Nonetheless, workdays are often scheduled in a way that makes it very difficult to get the proper amount of rest before a flight. Flights often leave in the early hours of the morning, and you'll often find yourself staying up all night. This type of rhythm is tough on the body. How much sleep do you require? How long can you go without sleep? Are you able to sleep on demand? Does your body require you to go to bed at the same time each night and wake up at the same time each morning? Are you the type of person who can nap?

Everybody is different. Many pilots I know aren't affected much by missing, postponed, and erratic sleep. Many others, myself included, find the schedule very tough on the body. There's nothing worse than lying in bed, desperately trying to get to sleep, knowing you have to be up at 3:30 a.m. the next morning. It's also very difficult to remain alert at 4 a.m. after being awake for up to eighteen hours—all while your passengers sleep soundly in their comfortable seats behind you. Fatigue can be deadly. In the Comair crash in Lexington, KY in 2006, the pilots were fatigued and mistakenly attempted to take off on the wrong runway. If the pilots had been more alert, there is a good chance the pilots would have caught the mistake before it was too late.

Strange sleep schedules are not limited to pilots. There are other jobs where you work odd hours or work long hours without sleep. In fact, pilots are fortunate in that there are specific duty-day requirements that limit the time pilots are allowed to work and require a fixed amount of rest between flights. Doctors, for example, often have to work nights on-call on top of working regular days in the hospital, and they don't have any regulation on the maximum number of hours they're allowed to work. Regardless, you need to know what your body is capable of.

Can You Work 14-hour Days?

On top of some crazy sleep schedules, being a pilot often requires you to work long hours. The maximum amount of time a pilot can work is fourteen hours in a row (not counting times when you can extend your duty-day for unforeseen circumstances). When you consider the average workday is eight or nine hours, adding another five or six hours to that can make for a very long workday. Although how often you will work a full 14 hours will vary with the job and your employer, it is something that you need to be able to handle. Doing it while staying in a reasonably good mood is also important to keep a good working relationship with your other crew members. It is often at the end of these long days where there inevitably ends up being complicated scheduling issues.

14-hour days can often go by surprisingly quickly. You're spending the time doing something you love, going to different cities around the world, and the scenery changes right before your eyes— not something most office workers get to experience!

Can You Handle Job Instability?

The economic realities of the new millennium are such that most people starting out in the work force will change jobs or even careers numerous times. It's very unlikely that a person will keep a single job from the time they leave school until the day they retire. In aviation, the industry tends to be even more unpredictable than in other sectors of the economy. Airlines are constantly emerging and disappearing. Existing airlines will have hiring booms and then a few years later lay off all the pilots they just hired! It can be disconcerting to constantly worry about the safety of your job.

There's a common saying that in Japanese, the word for crisis is the same as for opportunity (and not crisortunity like Homer Simpson claims). While I don't know if that is true, there is some truth in the meaning. Often when something bad happens, especially in employment situations, after a bit of a tough time, things usually end up working out for the best. The airline that I was flying for before I went back to school shut down just a few months after I left. It was frustrating for all my colleagues who had lost their jobs, however, for most of them, things have worked out for the best. Although most were unemployed for a short time, most ended up finding new and better opportunities.

Some people are able to go with the flow better than others. For some, being unemployed is not only financially uncertain, but also leads to extreme amounts of emotional distress. As I mentioned near the beginning of the book, I think no matter what your take on life is, having a back-up plan is a really good idea should you choose to become a pilot. For someone who would find losing a job ridiculously stressful, you've now put in place a safety-net, and for those who don't stress quite as much, you have an opportunity to pursue other areas.

It's something that unfortunately you have to take into consideration when choosing a career. Do you want to know exactly where you're going to be working for the rest of your life, or are you satisfied in knowing that a job you have now may not last you forever?

Hangar Talk – Things to Think About

I think that being a pilot is the best job in the world, but there is continuous training. Now a pilot has to be willing to live anywhere from Thompson, Manitoba to Seoul, South Korea.

—Chris Knox, A340/A330 Captain – Air Canada

Make SURE this is exactly what you want to do. DON'T do it for the money or you will be very disappointed for at least the first four years. Plan on living in the north and dealing with northern people— they're your bread and butter and you are NOT better than them, no matter what you think. Life is what you make of it. Enjoy the adventure of the journey of life. What seems like hell on earth right now may be one of the memories you look back on fondly in the future…try to make the best of the situation you're in.

—Chris Prodaehl, King Air Captain – Fast Air

Don't do it for the money—jobs that pay well in aviation are really rare. Make sure your partner is independent or she'll probably eventually leave you. Be prepared to miss a lot of special occasions because of your job, and be prepared to cancel a lot of plans because of your job. That being said, it's the best job on the planet. My office view beats anyone else's.

—Shane Murphy, Corporate C550 Captain

If there is ANYTHING you think you would like to do other than fly airplanes, go do that instead. Make some money, then buy a plane for fun. You really have to be a fanatic to put up with this industry.

—Mike Stefanski, B1900D First Officer – Central Mountain Air

Flying can be an incredibly rewarding and a fun career, but it will require a large investment of time and money on your part. Jobs aren't handed out like candy. You have to work for them. Ensure those in your life (especially significant others) are ready to support you. It may be years before you can be financially self-sufficient again. Once the decision is made, though, jump in with both feet and hang on for the ride of your life.

—Rob Nabieszko, PC-12 First Officer – LCE Aviation

The Flying Disease

Don't misinterpret these questions as negativity towards aviation. I believe it's important for you to know all the information there is to know, but I still believe that being a pilot is one of the finest jobs you can have. While writing this book I sent out a questionnaire to various pilots, and it's their answers you've been reading in the Hangar Talk sections. One of the questions I asked was: "Any other thoughts you'd give to a new pilot, or someone considering becoming a pilot?" One pilot, who wishes to remain anonymous, replied:

"Don't. Run far away. If you have enough money to afford to become a pilot, you are doing well enough to fly recreationally. If you don't have enough money then you can't afford to become a pilot. Borrow? Are you NUTS? You won't make minimum wage for the first couple of years. Go get a real job, and fly for fun."

Not a very positive review. However, when asked why she became a pilot, the same pilot responded *"I was hooked on aviation. Flying for a living seemed like a better idea than working a different job and spending all my money on flying."* This same pilot also writes a comprehensive blog documenting her daily flying adventures and continues to fly years after she started. There's something about the job and about flying that's addictive and keeps people pursuing the dream of flying.

The job of being a pilot is unique from almost every other job. You don't have a set schedule. You don't have a punch clock. You don't have to sit in a little cubicle without windows; your little cubicle has lots of windows! People are genuinely interested in the type of job you do. The stories you tell about your day at work will usually be more exciting than anybody else's. Instead of having to type reports or attend meetings, a pilot's task for the day is to fly an expensive and complex aircraft to a different city. Which sounds more interesting to you: reviewing personnel reports, or flying to Vegas?

Flying itself is a feeling like no other. Being in control of an aircraft flying through the air is one of the most amazing feelings. Just think—a hundred years ago, before the Wright brothers took that historic flight, no one was an airline pilot. For thousands of years, no human was able to experience the feeling of being in control of an aircraft. It really is a rush. I personally liked flying on days when the weather wasn't very good. After taking off and flying into the clouds, you break out through the top of the clouds into glorious sunlight. As you break out, you can sense that you're moving extremely quickly, and it reinforces all the guilty pleasures—I would often find myself thinking of all the people below, stuck in traffic on a cloudy day while I soared above the clouds. It's at this moment that most pilots think either (a) I have the best job in the world and/or (b) I can't believe I get paid to do this!

The Future of Aviation

It's an exciting time for the aviation industry. There are two new developments that may make quite an impact on the industry as a whole. One is the introduction of the double-decker Airbus A380, and the second is the development of the very light jet (VLJ). For almost forty years, the Boeing 747 has been the largest passenger aircraft in service, but in 2005, Airbus started flight-testing its new Airbus A380 jet. The A380, expected to enter service in late 2007 or early 2008, will overtake the 747 as the largest passenger jet in the world, with room for up to 555 passengers with later models expected to be able to hold up to 800 passengers. While industry insiders are no doubt excited about the launching of the world's largest airliner, it remains to be seen if the larger jet will make a difference in the way the industry operates. While the possibility of carrying more passengers per flight could lower costs, having such a large plane could cause problems at airport terminals, especially with boarding. It already takes a fair amount of time to load three-hundred passengers on the current wide-body aircraft, and almost doubling that passenger load is sure to cause sizeable delays. To combat this concern, some airports are constructing double-decker boarding gates. It will be interesting to see the results.

The A380 in Vancouver
Photo by Mike Stefanski

While the A380 is increasing the size of passenger jets, some analysts believe the development of VLJs will have an even greater impact on the way the industry operates. The very light jet is a name given to a category of jets that are smaller than the current smallest business jet. The big draw of these VLJs is that they offer private operators jet performance at a price only slightly above that of many small twin-engine piston and turbo-prop aircraft. The development of these VLJs could result in two separate trends that may change the make-up of the industry. The first trend is due to the low price: small companies or wealthy individuals may find that owning a jet is now more economically feasible. The result—more people will be able to own their own jet aircraft. The second trend is the potential increase of air taxi operators. The air taxis could offer their services from smaller airports via charter or scheduled services. Because of their low purchasing and operating costs, it could be possible to remain profitable with only a few passengers aboard. Both trends may offer increased employment opportunities for pilots, but it's still too early to speculate on the final outcome.

An increase in the number of very light jets could pose a problem—a clogging of the air traffic control system. Even now, the busier airports experience traffic delays. This could be exacerbated by the introduction of hundreds of very light jets into the system. There has been some development in regards to increasing the capacity of the air traffic control system, however, the outcome still remains to be seen.

Final Thoughts

Deciding on a career is one of the most important choices you'll make in your lifetime. A job isn't the only means to measure the success of a person's life, but your chosen profession will have a great impact on how you live your life, and how much you'll enjoy your life. As a result, it's not a decision that should be made lightly. There are many factors that you must examine about your own personality and the job itself. No matter what job you do, you're not going to enjoy every single day. There will be good days and bad days, and the hope is that the good days will far outweigh the bad. It's also important to look at what the potential schedules and benefits will be. While money isn't everything, many people find it difficult to do what they enjoy doing while being flat broke. At the same time, what good is having a wonderful job with a good salary if you don't have any spare time to enjoy it?

Becoming a pilot is not an easy process. It requires hard work and sacrifice. It requires being able to plan things far in advance and it also requires that you be ready to make a potentially life-altering decision at a moment's notice. It requires a lot of patience and a bit of luck thrown in for good measure. But what fun would life be without a challenge?

In this book I've attempted to portray a balanced view of the challenges and benefits of becoming a pilot. I've tried not to "sell" it. Instead, I've attempted to pass along the information required for you to make an informed decision about choosing aviation as a career. I highly recommend you talk to as many different people and pilots as possible before deciding your future. Becoming a pilot is a job, and for many, it can be a great job. Just go into it with your eyes open.

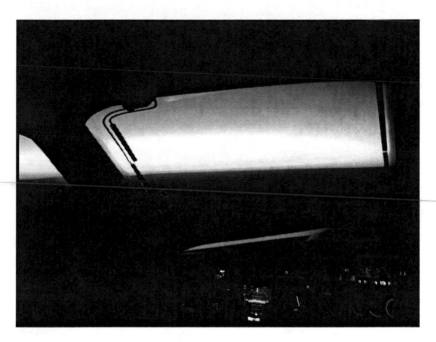

Sunset in a PC-12
photo by Adam Van Dusen

APPENDIX ONE: SAMPLE AVIATION RÉSUMÉ

Jane Smith
123 Main St. Barrie, ON. L5S 1Z7
H: (905) 555-9233 C: (905) 555-1234
e-mail: jsmith@gmail.ca

Aviation Experience

Total Time	PIC	Multi	Multi-PIC	Float
240	150	35	3	50

Licence & Ratings
- Canadian Commercial Pilot's Licence
- Multi-Engine IFR rating
- Float rating
- IATRA written

Types Flown
B58 Baron, C185 (floats), various light singles

Employment History
May 2006 – Oct 2006:   Dock Hand
                        Water Airways, Vancouver BC

June 2005 – April 2006 Ramp Attendant
                        Northern Pike Air, Stoney Rapids, SK

Education

2003 – 2005   **Bill & Ted's Aviation College** – Aviation
Diploma
- graduated with Honours

1999 – 2003   **Bovine University** – Bachelor of Arts
- Majored in livestock management
- Minored in forklift maintenance

References

Doug Jones – First Officer, Phoenix Airlines (519) 555-4321
Bob MacKenzie – Flight Instructor, Bill & Ted's Aviation College
(905) 555-3389

Note About Résumé

This is just a basic example of what needs to be included on a résumé. I kept a number of sections quite short because of the smaller page size—you'll have more room on your full-page résumé. Please keep in mind that this is just a starter guide. There's a fair amount of leeway in how you'll want to present your information to a potential employer. Be creative, but at the same time, make sure that you present all the required information neatly and concisely. It wouldn't hurt to briefly expand upon duties at a previous job, especially if they are relevant to the job for which you are applying.

APPENDIX TWO: AIR CANADA SAMPLE INTERVIEW QUESTIONS

Note: These are a sampling of questions that pilots have been asked during recent interviews. This is not an exhaustive list nor is it intended to be the sole study guide for interview preparation. There are separate resources for interview preparation available. These questions are meant as a guide of things to consider while proceeding in your career.

Air Canada

- ✈ What do you expect from Air Canada?
- ✈ What can you bring to Air Canada?
- ✈ Why should Air Canada hire you?
- ✈ Do you have a preference of base?
- ✈ Are you willing to relocate?
- ✈ Do you want to be a cruise relief pilot or an Embraer F/O?
- ✈ Does your company know that you're here?
- ✈ Do you have any questions for us?

Personal

- ✈ Tell us about yourself.
- ✈ How did you get interested in aviation?
- ✈ What are your strengths?
- ✈ What are your weaknesses? How do they affect you and how are you trying to improve them?
- ✈ What is your greatest accomplishment?

✈ What was the hardest thing you've ever done?
✈ How do you deal with change?
✈ How do you handle stress?
✈ Have you ever hurt someone's feelings? What was the situation and how did you deal with it?
✈ How do you deal with someone you don't like at work?
✈ Describe a problem or dispute that you had with a colleague.
✈ Why didn't you finish a particular level of education?
✈ Tell us about a time when you were over-confident?

Operational

✈ Have you had to deal with a difficulty in the cockpit and how did you manage it?
✈ How do you involve the crew?
✈ How well do you complete training?
✈ What kind of Captain would you be?
✈ What would your leadership style be as a Captain?
✈ What is CRM, and how does a good Captain use CRM?
✈ Have you ever failed a check-ride or required additional training?
✈ What traits make a good airline Captain, and which of those traits do you possess?
✈ What was the toughest decision you've ever had to make in relation to aviation?
✈ Have you ever scared yourself?

Past Experience

✈ Tell us about your most memorable aviation experience.
✈ Describe your aviation history.
✈ Why do you want to leave your current company?
✈ If you could change one thing at your company, what would it be?
✈ How would your former supervisors describe you?
✈ How could your present company improve their CRM training?
✈ Tell us some things that you didn't like about your last job.
✈ Tell us about a time when you used teamwork to get something done well?

APPENDIX THREE: WESTJET SAMPLE INTERVIEW QUESTIONS

Note: These are a sampling of questions that pilots have been asked during recent interviews. This is not an exhaustive list nor is it intended to be the sole study guide for interview preparation. There are separate resources for interview preparation available. These questions are meant as a guide of things to consider while proceeding in your career.

WestJet

- ✈ Why do you want to work for WestJet? What prompted you to apply now?
- ✈ What qualities / skills will you bring to WestJet?
- ✈ What do you know about WestJet? (fleet, number of employees etc.)
- ✈ What did you do to prepare for this interview?
- ✈ Does your current employer know that you're here? Can we contact them?
- ✈ What do you think are the roles of various other employees at WestJet? (Captain, First Officer, Flight Attendant, dispatcher etc.)

Teamwork

- ✈ How do you treat your co-workers?
- ✈ Tell us about a time when ....

✈ you worked with a team that you enjoyed / disliked.

✈ you had to solve a problem as a member of a team.

✈ you went along with a team's decision even though you didn't agree with it.

✈ you contributed to working in or creating a team environment.

Problem Solving / Decision Making

✈ What process do you use to solve a problem?

✈ Tell us about a time when...

✈ you used good judgement and logic to solve a problem.

✈ you used fact finding skills to solve a problem.

✈ you used initiative / creativity to solve a problem.

✈ you missed an easy solution to a problem.

✈ you had to think on your feet to solve a problem.

✈ How do you make decisions?

✈ What was a difficult decision you've had to make in the past?

✈ Tell us about a time....

✈ you had to make a quick decision.

✈ you used common sense to make a decision

✈ you had to do something that you weren't comfortable with.

✈ you had an emergency in the airplane.

✈ you had to make an operational decision.

✈ you made a decision but then took a different direction after already starting your first decision.

✈ you had to take a leadership role to make a decision.

✈ you recognized a potential problem and the steps you took to resolve it.

✈ you had to make a decision and were accountable for the results.

Communication / Conflict Resolution

✈ Tell us about a time when ...

✈ you disagreed with a co-worker. Were you able to find a solution?
✈ you had to work with someone you didn't get along with.
✈ you had to apologize to a co-worker.
✈ you were (not) able to successfully deal with another co-worker.
✈ you had to defuse a situation.
✈ you changed somebody's mind.
✈ as a leader you had to resolve a conflict.
✈ you established credibility through your actions.

→ How do you deal with flying with an unhappy crew?
→ What's your typical process for solving conflict?
→ How do you attempt to lighten the mood at work?

Customer Service

→ Tell us about a time when...

✈ you went above the call of duty for a customer.
✈ you had to deal with an unhappy / rude / unruly customer.
✈ you provided great customer service.

Personal

→ What are some of your weaknesses that you need to work on?
→ What is your biggest accomplishment?
→ What are your personal / professional standards that you follow?
→ How do you work under pressure?
→ How do you know if you've done a job well?
→ Tell us about a time when...

✈ you had too many things to do and you were required to prioritise your tasks.
✈ you had a stressful situation and how you dealt with it.
✈ you used humour to reduce stress.

✈ you set a personal goal and were (not) able to achieve it.

✈ you showed airmanship.

✈ you were unhappy with your performance in a situation.

✈ What was your least favourite job? Why?

✈ What do you like / dislike / hate about your current job?

AUTHOR BIOGRAPHY

James Ball was born and raised in Toronto, Ontario where, after an inspiring flight in the jump seat of an Airbus A320, he enrolled in aviation at Seneca College. He graduated with an Aviation and Flight Technology Diploma in 2001 along with certification as a Commercial Pilot and a Multi-Engine IFR rating. Following graduation, he moved to Thompson, MB where he worked for a small regional airline. Beginning his aviation career in a non-flying position on the ramp loading bags and cargo he paid his dues before getting his first flying position as First Officer on an Air Ambulance. He went on to become both a Captain & Training Captain on charter aircraft. While in Thompson, he also spent time working as a substitute teacher for the School District of Mystery Lake.

In 2005, James returned to school where he completed a Bachelor of Arts in Geography at McMaster University in Hamilton, Ontario. Currently, James is studying law at Dalhousie University in Halifax, Nova Scotia. Since returning to school, James has kept current with developments in the aviation industry and continues to fly recreationally when time and finances permit. In his spare time, he enjoys traveling, playing hockey, squash and golf and attempting to play something that resembles music with his bass guitar.

Writing on Stone Press is currently accepting manuscripts and query letters for a variety of non-fiction books.

We are especially seeking authors for our Canadian Career Series in the professions of Accounting, Dentistry, Chiropractic, Education, Architect, Engineer, Veterinarian and Pharmacist who have recently graduated from or are about to graduate from these programs.

Please forward your inquiries to:
Writing on Stone Press
Box 259
Raymond, Alberta
T0K 2S0

or fax us at 403-752-4815

Please read our submission guidelines at
http://www.writingonstone.ca

At Writing on Stone Press, we strive to produce quality books for our audiences. If you have noticed any errors in this publication, please let us know so that we can make any necessary corrections for future printings. Thank you.